# I Speak for My Slave Sister

### THE LIFE OF ABBY KELLEY FOSTER

# WOMEN OF AMERICA
## Milton Meltzer, EDITOR

# THE BRUMBACK LIBRARY

## OF VAN WERT COUNTY

## VAN WERT, OHIO

MARGARET HOPE BACON

# I Speak for
# My Slave Sister

THE LIFE OF ABBY KELLEY FOSTER

*Illustrated with Photographs*

Thomas Y. Crowell Company · New York

CD RG MK KW BB VG

*Copyright © 1974 by Margaret Hope Bacon*

All rights reserved. Except for use in a review,

Designed by Elliot Epstein
Picture Editor: R. Lynn Goldberg

Manufactured in the United States of America

Library of Congress Cataloging in Publication Data
Bacon, Margaret Hope.
I speak for my slave sister:
the life of Abby Kelley Foster.
(Women of America)
SUMMARY: A biography of Abby Kelley Foster,
pacifist, abolitionist, and campaigner for women's rights
in the 1840s.
1. Foster, Abigail Kelley, 1810–1887—Juv.
lit. 2. Slavery in the United States—Anti-
slavery movements—Juv. lit. 3. Abolitionists—Juv. lit.
[1. Foster, Abigail Kelley, 1810–1887. 2. Abolitionists.
3. Women's rights] I. Title.
E449.F742B32       322.4'4'0924   [B]   [92]       74-4042

ISBN 0-690-00515-6

1 2 3 4 5 6 7 8 9 10

*For Peggy and Betsy*

# Acknowledgments

IF Abby Kelley Foster had not been a prolific letter writer—and if her many letters to friends and colleagues had not been saved—it would have been impossible to write this book. In providing me with microfilms and photocopies, in permitting me to quote from the documents consulted, a whole host of research librarians have aided me in making it possible to piece together the tale. The American Antiquarian Society and the Worcester Historical Society have provided the bulk of the correspondence, but there has been a great deal of helpful material, too, from the Boston Public Library, the Library of Columbia University, the Women's Archives at Radcliffe, the Library of Congress, the Historical Society of Pennsylvania.

A very special word must be said for the staff of several Quaker libraries: The Friends Historical Library at Swarthmore College, the Peace Collection, also at Swarthmore; the Quaker Collection at Haverford College, and the Archives of the New England Yearly Meeting. Without the help of the staff of these libraries I should have been lost. I must refer to Barbara Curtis, Jane Rittenhouse, Eleanor Maier, Thyra Jane Foster and Bernice Nichols for their special assistance and kindness.

Thanks are also due to Dr. George D. Carter of the University of Wisconsin for his help and encouragement, to Allen Bacon for his patience and support, and to Beth Binford and Wendy Waloff for typing.

# Contents

A Judith there, turned Quakeress
Sits Abby in her modest dress
Serving a table quietly
As if that mild and downcast eye
Flashed never, with its scorn intense,
More than Medea's eloquence.
So the same force which shakes its dread
Far-blazing locks o'er Aetna's head,
Along the wires in silence fares
And messages of commerce bears
No nobler gift of heart and brain
No life more white from spot or stain
Was e'er on Freedom's altar laid
Than hers—the simple Quaker maid.

from *Letter from Boston*, JAMES RUSSELL LOWELL

# I Speak for
# My Slave Sister

## THE LIFE OF ABBY KELLEY FOSTER

# Foreword

WHEN people thought about the women's rights movement in the 1840s, one name came to mind: Abby Kelley.

Abby was a schoolteacher from Lynn, Massachusetts, a Quaker of Irish descent, and an abolitionist. Described as the prettiest and most fiery woman in the antislavery movement, she was also the most controversial. She insisted on speaking to mixed audiences of men and women, when this was taboo, and in asserting her right to work against slavery not as a woman, but as a human being.

For this crime, she was the target of scathing sermons and editorials. Wherever she spoke, ugly crowds gathered and threw rotten eggs and insults at her. She didn't like it, but she kept going, and won for herself among her admirers the name of Joan of Arc.

All her life, Abby continued to act on the belief that men and women are equal. She entered upon a marriage contract that specified that equality. She shared with her husband the jobs of raising their daughter and running their farm. She traveled all over the country, taking care of herself, even though she was criticized for doing so.

Later, she scrimped to send her daughter to college, decried the idea that marriage was the only career for women, and worked for suffrage for women. In her old age she refused to pay taxes on her farm because she didn't have the right to vote.

Yet Abby's name has been lost in the mists of history. Partly this is because she was a radical, too uncompromising to work long and well with any organization. Though she was a source of inspiration to Lucy Stone, Susan B. Anthony, and many other leaders of the women's rights movement, she played only a minor role in the first associations.

But also, Abby was a woman over one hundred years ahead of her day. A pacifist, or nonresister, she opposed all war, refused to recognize the authority of the state, and distrusted politicians. She searched for the economic base for social problems and called for a breakup of concentrated wealth. She ate only natural foods, was interested in communes, wore pants when it suited her.

Her ideas, which sounded so outlandish then, seem contemporary today. We see in hindsight that she was often right when she refused to compromise. If there had been many more like her, the Civil War might not have been fought, Reconstruction would have been far more just, and our nation spared many decades of agony over the question of racial justice.

In fact, Abby sounds like a member of the dissident movement that grew out of the protest against the war in Vietnam. She confronted many of the same responses, and had the same impact on the society of her day. She believed you had to separate yourself from a system that sold women into slavery, just as war protesters have believed you must separate yourself from a system that bombs villages in Indochina.

Reading about her 130 years later, we can learn to better understand ourselves and our times.

# I

## *Beginnings*

BORN to become a militant symbol of women's rights, Abby
Kelley came into the world as a seventh daughter in a day
when sons were highly valued. Doubtless her parents had
been hoping for a boy. Wing Kelley needed boys to help him
till the rocky soil of his farm on the slopes of a mountain in
central Massachusetts. He already had six girls around the
house; two by a former marriage, four in rapid succession
since his marriage to his present wife, Diana Daniels.

Wing, however, was a gay and cheerful man, and Diana
believed in accepting the Lord's will without complaint.
When the new baby was born on January 15, 1811, they
comforted themselves that she was at least sound and healthy,
named her Abigail, and called in her admiring older sisters to
take a peek.

Abby's arrival came at a happy time in the life of her
parents. Despite the lack of boys, Wing had prospered as a
farmer in recent years. In the tiny nearby town of Pelham he
was well-respected and well-liked. Once he had been chosen to

serve on the local school board, and once named a selectman, a village governing official. He had many friends and liked to bring them home to his quiet wife and many daughters.

On First Days, when the snow was not too deep, the Kelleys hitched up and drove to the small Pelham Friends Meeting house. They were both members of the Society of Friends, or Quakers—Wing of Irish, Diana of English descent. Both the Kelleys and the Danielses had come to the colonies in the 1750s, and both had settled in Massachusetts and prospered there, despite some hostility from their neighbors.

The Bay Colony was never the friendliest place for Quakers. In the 1650s the Puritans had tried to drive the Quakers out, fearing them as religious heretics. When a handful insisted on exercising their religious liberty to speak, they were hanged on Boston Common. Later the Quakers made themselves unpopular in wartime by refusing to pay war taxes or train for the militia. During the Revolutionary War they not only refused to support the patriots but began an agitation for Massachusetts to give up her slaves. Quaker families like the Kelleys who survived all this learned to stick by their principles and ignore public opinion. Abby was born to a rich heritage of dissent.

Shortly after Abby's birth, a Daniels kinsman offered to sell the Kelleys a hundred-acre farm on the eastern outskirts of Worcester, a larger town forty miles to the east. The prospect pleased Diana very much. She had been born in Mendon, Massachusetts, a small town south of Worcester, and all her relatives still lived in that vicinity. Hoping some day to return, Diana had kept up her membership in Uxbridge

Friends Meeting, a few miles from Mendon, and had registered the births of her children there.

Though he had prospered in Pelham, Wing doubtless wanted to please his wife. He accepted the new farm and in May, when the spring muds were dry, he piled his daughters and household belongings onto several carts, ordered his hired men to round up the cattle, and traveled the forty miles east over rutted roads.

Set in a valley along rolling hills, watered by the Blackstone River, Worcester in 1811 was a pretty and prosperous town. Large homes of brick built in the Georgian style lined its wide, tree-shaded streets. Although not much industry had yet developed, there were several sawmills and gristmills in operation, and farmers from the fertile lands of the Massachusetts plateau came into town to conduct business.

The Kelleys' new farm, near the Grafton road, was a lovely place of rolling pastures and woodland. Here they continued to prosper and to produce children. In 1813 their only son, Albert, was born, and in 1819 a final daughter, Lucy.

Young Abby may have resented the new arrivals. She was deeply attached to her father, and was probably jealous of his pleasure in the arrival of a son when she was only two years old. In later life she never mentioned Albert, and was markedly critical of Lucy. It was to her older sisters that she felt close.

As the mother of a growing brood, Diana Kelley was busy from morning to night. There was cheese and butter to churn from the milk, bread to make, heavy cloth—linsey-woolsey—to weave on a loom for the winter clothes, stockings to knit, geese to feed, candles to dip, and a hundred other chores. When Abby was a baby, stoves were not in general use, and women had to cook over an open hearth. Clothes were washed by hand and spread out on bushes to dry. Even clotheslines were regarded as a newfangled invention.

To help her feed and clothe her family, Diana had her older daughters and a succession of hired girls. Supervising the little girls in their chores was more of a problem than a help. When Abby grew frail, and the doctor suggested that she needed more fresh air, Diana was glad to let her roam the farm at will.

Unsupervised, Abby learned all sorts of things which little girls at that time were not supposed to do. She climbed trees, straddled fences, and skipped stones across the pond. When her sisters and cousins teased her and called her a tomboy, she flashed back at them that she would hate to spend the time indoors, forever playing with dolls.

Still, there were limits to what girls could do. When the streams and ponds froze over, and the boys went skating, a girl had to stay off the ice unless some boy condescended to offer to pull her around behind him by a stick. Abby thought it was a humiliation to be treated so, and went off to slide down the snowy hills on barrel staves, alone if need be.

But if little Abby was a rebel outdoors, she knew how to be good as gold when she went with her parents and her many sisters to the Worcester Friends Meeting. From the age of three she probably had her own little Quaker bonnet and was expected to sit still for as much as an hour at a time while the Quakers conducted their silent meeting for worship.

Although women sat on one side of the meetinghouse and men on the other, both were regarded as equal in the sight of

God. The Quakers had no paid ministers: They believed that God could speak directly to each man or each woman. In the silence of the meeting a member would rise to give a message which had been "opened" to him or her. A person who spoke often was recorded by the meeting as a minister. There were as many women as men ministers, and Abby grew up thinking it was perfectly natural and right for a woman to preach to men. Only years later did she discover how the rest of the world in those days was opposed to this practice.

As earnestly as she could, Abby learned to wait for the Lord to speak to her. She was a religious little girl, who at first pictured God as a kindly old man who sat up in the attic. Later she learned he was a spirit who reproved her when she was naughty and would guide her life if she put it in his hands. It was important, the Quakers believed, to await the Lord's leading and to trust that if something were divinely guided the "way would open."

Abby's mother was a far stricter Quaker than her father. It was Diana who disciplined the children, insisted that they use *thee* and *thou* and wear only plain clothes, heard their prayers, and taught them to believe in the Inner Light. Abby adored her father, but it was from her mother that she got her determination and her driving conscience.

Another area where Abby shone was school. Children in those days started school as early as three, tagging along with older sisters and brothers to the one-room schoolhouse. Here, hard-pressed teachers set the little ones to learning the alphabet or working their samplers, while the older grades recited their lessons.

It was an age of memorization. The schools for young children were called grammar schools, and each child was expected to commit to heart all the rules of English grammar, often without having the least idea what the rules meant. Small children droned, "of, to, for, by, with, in, into, within, without, over, under, through, above, below, before, behind, beneath, on or upon, among, after, against," for months before they were taught to use a single preposition.

Once the rules of grammar were memorized, there were maps and multiplication tables to commit to heart. Occasionally, as a treat, poetry was added to the curriculum. At times, the whole classroom would hum with recitation. At other times, it would be quiet except for the scratch of slates, as little children worked on penmanship and arithmetic sums.

Teachers came and teachers went, often without much more training than the oldest child in the school. There were few public schools as such. It was often the most ambitious parents in the community who hired the teacher. Schoolrooms were primitive, heated by a small wood stove or even an open hearth in winter. Water came from a pump in the front yard, and there were outdoor privies.

Abby loved it all and admired most of her teachers, though she flinched when an angry master caned one of the big boys. Slowly an ambition began to form in her mind: Some day she herself would become a teacher and discipline the children by touching their minds and their hearts, rather than cracking their knuckles.

By fourteen she had completed the highest grade offered in Worcester. She was a slim, earnest girl with a ramrod-straight back, heavy chestnut hair, bright pink cheeks, white skin, and blue eyes. She had no sense of humor and was bewildered when told a joke, but she liked to see others laugh. She was often teased for her earnestness and for her one great failing:

She could never keep a secret but straightway had to repeat it "in confidence" to a friend.

None of her older sisters had gone further than grammar school, but Abby had greater ambitions. The Friends School in Providence, Rhode Island, founded in 1779, had reopened in 1819 and was accepting both girls and boys, offering them the equivalent of a modern high-school education. The idea that boys and girls should receive an equal education was another peculiarity of Quakers at this time. The more Abby heard about it, the more determined she became to attend.

But where would she get the money for tuition? Certainly not from her parents, who were beginning to have financial difficulties. Wing had sold the farm on the Grafton road in 1822, buying a larger one on the west side of Worcester, near Tatnuck Hill. The second farm, though larger, was less fertile, and Wing supplemented his income by operating a sawmill. All spare cash went into the enterprise.

Instead, Abby borrowed money from a married older sister and enrolled herself at the Friends School. Although Providence was only forty miles away, it seemed a great distance in those days, and girls as young as Abby did not often leave home. Everyone admired her pluck and her determination, but doubtless a few of the neighbors thought the Kelleys touched in the head to permit such nonsense.

The Friends School was run with strict Quaker plainness at the time Abby attended it. Plainness in speech meant using only *thee* and *thou;* plainness in apparel meant nothing added for show, such as an extra row of buttons or a rolled collar. There was no music or dancing. For recreation the students skipped rope or played a game of battledore with paddles and a shuttlecock.

The school day began at dawn. The students slept in a long open dormitory, or chamber, two to a bed, the girls' wing at one end of the building, the boys' at another. At the foot of the bed was a little horsehide trunk for each student, containing all his possessions. After they were up and dressed, students marched decorously, two by two, in silence to the collecting room, where they awaited the breakfast bell.

In the diningroom, boys and girls sat at separate long tables, and were allowed to converse only in whispers. Breakfast consisted of bread and sweetened coffee, with sometimes the addition of salt fish. Morning school lasted until twelve; then came dinner—soup, boiled potatoes, salt pork, sometimes pudding—followed by two hours of outdoor play. Lessons started again at two. The young scholars studied grammar, reading, writing, arithmetic, and geography, continuing with their earlier education. Again, the secret was to memorize. By 4:30 P.M. it was time for a short break, then supper—called tea—followed by two hours of grammar. The younger students went to bed at eight, the older ones at nine.

In this Spartan régime Abby thrived. She was not a brilliant scholar, but she had a clear, logical mind, and she was determined. Sometimes she studied so hard that she broke out in a sweat, as though she had been running. Her teachers were delighted by her industry, and she began to rank high in her class.

After a year at Friends, Abby at fifteen was considered perfectly qualified to teach a grammar school. She had not completed all the courses she wanted to take, but she needed to repay the debt to her older sister. With her teachers' recommendation in hand, she therefore got a job teaching in a small school near Worcester.

Facing her first classroom of youngsters must have been an exciting moment for young Abby. There were children of all ages, from lisping three-year-olds to great hulking boys of fourteen and fifteen, some older—and certainly bigger—than Abby herself. How was she going to make them mind her, if she did not use a stick?

The answer was, by moral force. Though young, Abby was stern. She knew the difference between right and wrong, never flinched from duty, and expected others to behave as she did. She had a strong voice, which she did not mind raising if it were necessary to make herself heard. By lecturing her pupils, she shamed the slow scholars into learning, the naughty ones into good behavior. Soon she kept perfect order by her mere presence in front of them.

After a year of teaching school, Abby had been able to pay back her sister and save a little besides. Once again she set out for Providence and more months of hard study at the Friends School. She stayed again until her funds ran out, then got another school to teach. Alternating work and study in this way, she continued at Friends until 1829 and left at the age of eighteen, having completed the highest level of education available for young women anywhere in New England.

Meanwhile, things were not going well at home. Wing's financial troubles increased, and he was forced to sell over thirty acres of his best pastureland. The older sisters were by now all married. Abby decided to return to Worcester to teach and contribute her share to the family income.

She was young, she was successful, she was striking—some said beautiful. She had a graceful figure and liked to dance; though this conflicted with Quaker discipline, her parents encouraged her to attend the sedate dancing parties for young

men and women held in Worcester at this time. She was fond
of dress, and spent some of her hard-earned money on clothes.
Quakers of the day often varied the simplicity of their
costume by choosing rich silks and satins in subtle, quiet
colors. The women always wore a white kerchief about their
necks. Abby was especially vain about keeping hers spotless
and dainty. She did not lack for young men to take her to
parties, but she evidently did not encourage their attentions.
Her mind was on other things: her teaching, her parents, her
duties at Friends Meeting.

It looked for a time as though Abby were heading in a
perfectly respectable and predictable direction. She would be a
schoolteacher who stayed home with her parents and improved her mind. But then a new interest arose to claim her
attention and change the whole course of her life. That issue
was slavery.

# II

# *Birth of a Concern*

ABBY came to be concerned about slavery partly as a matter of inheritance. The Quakers had long been opposed to slavery, having been the first people to speak out against it in the seventeenth century, the first to give up their own slaves in the eighteenth, and the first to insist on emancipation in the Northern states. Quakers assumed they were still in the lead on this issue, and all Quaker children were taught to "pity the poor slave in his bondage" as soon as they could speak.

The Quakers had used an appeal to reason and to conscience to persuade their own members to give up slaves. The Pennsylvania Abolition Society, the world's first antislavery group, organized largely by Quakers in Philadelphia in 1775, was based on a belief that slave-owners could be gradually led to see the error of their ways. This persuasion was so gentle that for a time the society had more branches in the South than in the North.

By the 1820s, however, it was clear that slavery was not going to yield to rational argument. The invention of the cotton gin, a machine for removing seeds from cotton, made it possible for Southern plantation owners to process as much cotton as they could grow. The demand for huge gangs of slaves to work the cotton fields grew spectacularly in the Deep South, and other Southern states began to breed slaves and sell them south to fill the need. Shortly, the economy of most of the South became dependent upon slavery. If a man tried to free his slaves and swim against the tide, as some North Carolina Quakers did, he was soon bankrupt and ostracized by his neighbors.

Other sources of conflict were developing between the North and the South. In the North, industry was just beginning to develop. Northern businessmen wanted tariffs to protect these infant industries. Southerners sold some of their cotton to the weaving mills of New England, but they sold some also to Great Britain and bought cheap consumer goods in return. They benefited by free trade.

Since each slave was counted as three fifths of a person in representation in Congress, the more slaves and more slave-owning states there were, the more power the South had to oppose tariffs and to protect their other interests. The North needed more free states in order to pass national legislation favorable to its regional concerns. As a result, both North and South were determined that there be at least an equal number of slave-owning and free states in the Union. When Missouri was admitted as a slave-owning state in 1820, Maine was admitted as a free state, thus keeping the balance even. At the same time, the Missouri Compromise decreed that slavery would be excluded from all territory above the latitude $36°30'$.

The opponents of slavery at this time were in favor of

gradual emancipation, and many backed a scheme of colonization. This idea was to send the free blacks back to Africa, where a colony had already been established in Liberia. This would solve the problem in the United States, it was believed, while bringing the supposed benefits of white, Christian civilization to the African continent.

Abby may have first read about colonization in a newspaper called *The Genius of Universal Emancipation*, published in Maryland. She had begun, soon after leaving Friends School, to read a great deal on the subject of slavery. The fact that slave families were separated—that husbands were taken from their wives and children from their mothers—and sold down the river to the large cotton plantations in the Deep South upset her profoundly. Even worse was the discovery that white masters used young black women for sexual gratification. She imagined what it would be like to be a young black woman so used, and she felt a burning humiliation. The colonization scheme for a time seemed to her like the only way out. Let the blacks go back to Africa, since Americans were too wicked to treat them properly.

Then she went to a lecture which moved her deeply and changed the whole course of her life. The lecturer was William Lloyd Garrison; the subject of his discourse, the colonization scheme.

Garrison had worked as a reporter on *The Genius of Universal Emancipation*, and had agreed for a while with the concept of colonization. But then black friends in Baltimore had pointed out to him that the scheme was really serving not to free the slaves but to take free blacks back to Liberia. The slave-owners liked this development. While free blacks lived successfully in the North, they were a source of encouragement to slaves to escape. At the same time, by adapting to free American society, they were walking, talking proofs of the argument that there was no inherent difference of ability between the races.

In 1831 Garrison established his own paper, *The Liberator*, in Boston and began in its columns to attack colonization and to preach immediate emancipation. His tone was fiery, and he immediately established for himself a reputation as the radical of the antislavery movement.

Abby did not know what to expect when she went to hear him. Having read *The Liberator*, she might have anticipated a large, fierce man with bushy whiskers. Instead the figure that came to the podium was wispy, the face mild and sweet. Garrison, though young, was balding, wore rimless glasses, and smiled often. He did not look as though he could hurt a fly.

The Worcester Town Hall was filled to overflowing. Whether they agreed with him or not, people flocked to hear the famous Garrison. A deep hush fell as Garrison began his speech. Abby sat on the edge of her chair, breathless.

Garrison began mildly enough by describing how he had once believed in colonization, how he had begun to doubt it, and how examination of reports from the free African state of Liberia had confirmed his thinking.

"It can be demonstrated," he said, "that the American Colonization Society has inflicted a great injury upon the free and slave population; first, by strengthening the prejudices of the people—second, by discouraging the education of those who are free—and finally, by lulling the whole country into a deep sleep."

Was I one of those lulled? Abby wondered.

Garrison continued to describe how Liberia, instead of

being a Christian colony, was a place of "forts and murderous wars, rum and tobacco," and to suggest that most of the men who supported colonization did so with mixed motives: they either owned slaves or did business with slave-owners.

"In opposing the American Colonization Society, I have also counted the cost, and as clearly foreseen the formidable opposition which will be arrayed against me," Garrison concluded. "Many of the clergy are enlisted in its support; their influence is powerful. Men of wealth and elevated station are among its contributors; wealth and station are almost omnipotent. The press has been seduced into its support, the press is a potent engine. Moreover, the Society is artfully based upon and defended by popular prejudice; it takes advantage of wicked and preposterous opinions, and hence its success. These things grieve, they cannot deter me. 'Truth is mighty and will prevail.' It is able to make falsehood blush, and take from hypocrisy its mask, and annihilate prejudices, and overthrow persecution, and break every fetter."

There was a tremendous uproar at the end of his speech. Some clapped, but there was also hissing and booing. Abby left with the crowd, her head in a whirl. She saw that she had been among those deceived—that colonization was indeed a mask worn by selfish men to cover their real motives. She would never again, she promised herself, fail to look below the surface. She would be like Garrison and seek the truth, no matter what it cost her. His defiance of church and establishment spoke to her rebellious soul. She longed for an opportunity to prove her faithfulness under fire.

The opportunity was long in coming. Abby continued to be needed at home. Wing's financial difficulties increased. In 1835 he again sold his farm, at a loss, and bought a smaller one in Millbury, south of Worcester. Albert and Lucy had both followed Abby's example and gone to Friends School. While they, too, worked their way through, they were unable to contribute much to the household.

Then, in the spring of 1836, Abby was invited to take charge of a small Friends school in Lynn, Massachusetts, just outside of Boston. Her salary as head teacher would be larger than that which she earned in Worcester, and she would be able to send some home. It seemed like a good chance to get away and to do some independent reading and thinking.

Lynn was a seaport town, with bracing salt air and tall schooners lying at anchor in the harbor. The waterfront smelled of fish and tar, and resounded to the shouts and oaths of sailors. Above the harbor sat a sedate New England town, and beyond stretched miles of open fields.

The Friends school, of which Abby took charge, included fifty-six students in all. About 30 of them were in the primary grades, taught by Anna Breed Smith; the rest were under Abby's personal care. Tuition for the little ones was twelve and a half cents a week; for the older ones, one shilling. Abby took over her new duties easily and quickly, and soon had established a strong influence over the pupils. By December the visiting committee commented that "good order and improvement manifested have been much to their satisfaction."

In Lynn, Abby boarded with a congenial family and soon made a circle of friends—young women, unmarried like herself, many of them schoolteachers. Life fell quickly into a pattern: school from nine to two, perhaps a walk in the afternoon, time to write letters to relatives and to prepare lessons for the next day, supper, and evenings of work or parlor talk, where the women chatted about "pretty babies and new gowns and caps," as a friend of Abby's once commented sarcastically.

To escape this dull routine, Abby and her circle devoted their evening discussions to different topics. They read about phrenology, the new science of studying a person's character by examining the bumps on his head. They exchanged notes about Grahamism, the new fad for eating only natural foods and whole-wheat products, promoted by reformer Sylvester Graham. They talked about the new temperance movement, the new moral reform movement, the new peace movement. They read aloud to each other from the poems of Quaker abolitionist John Greenleaf Whittier.

But discussion was not enough for Abby. She had been overjoyed on arriving in Lynn to discover that there was an active group she could join. It was the Lynn Female Anti-Slavery Society, and she soon became its corresponding secretary. After years of longing, she was at last engaged in the battle.

That there should be such a thing as a female antislavery society, Abby apparently did not question at first. Women's activities were separate from those of men in almost every area of life. Even the Quakers, who allowed women to preach to men in meeting for worship, held separate men's and women's meetings for business. Although women had been present at the founding of the American Anti-Slavery Society in 1833, and a few had spoken to the group (after asking permission to do so), it had been considered entirely natural that separate women's groups should be organized for the day-to-day work of raising money, circulating petitions, and arranging meetings.

Abby was just becoming active in her new role with the

antislavery society when word came that Wing Kelley was desperately ill. She hurried home to his deathbed. The loss of her kindly father threw Abby into a deep depression. It took her a year to get "fully settled," she told her sister, and in the course of that year she delved more deeply into the religion of her childhood, experiencing the need "to look beyond earthly things for a support" and finding at last that "my heavenly Father is my refuge." As a result of this experience she was deepened, made more sensitive, and yearned more intensely for "way to open."

In March 1837, just a few months after her father's death, Abby felt led to address a letter to a fellow Quaker and a sister abolitionist, Angelina Grimké. Angelina and her older sister Sarah were making names for themselves as antislavery lecturers. Born of a wealthy, slave-owning South Carolina family, the two had moved north, joined the Society of Friends, and begun to denounce slavery on the basis of their personal childhood experiences. They were much in demand with female audiences, and occasionally a man would slip into the back of the room to hear them.

As the experience of the two Grimké sisters in antislavery circles broadened, they became more and more dissatisfied with the Society of Friends. They believed the Quakers were living on their past reputation and were little interested in accepting the blacks as equals. Blacks were either refused membership in the society or asked to sit on a special bench in the back of the meetinghouse. The Quakers were also suspicious of the new antislavery agitation. They advised their members to form their own Quaker antislavery societies and to "keep in the quiet."

Abby wrote Angelina, about whom she had read in *The*

*Liberator*, to assure her that things were not so bad in Massachusetts as they were in Philadelphia. The Lynn Quakers were sufficiently aroused to antislavery concerns that they could even bear Garrison. Since Lynn was in such a fine state, why did not the Grimké sisters pay the town a visit?

Angelina declined, but urged Abby to attend the first national Anti-Slavery Convention of American Women, to be held in New York in May.

Abby had never been out of Massachusetts and was such a pennypincher that the thought of a trip to far-off New York was doubtless upsetting at first. But her need to become active in the movement outweighed her timidity and penury. With a delegation of five other women, she made the trip by stagecoach and train.

New York City in 1838 was a bustling metropolis of 300,000, stretching all the way from Castle Gardens on the Battery to Greenwich Village. There were broad avenues full of the carriages of the wealthy; small, twisting lanes along which lived the poor; ships in harbor at the waterfront. Abby had never been in so big a city. Unfortunately, there was no time for sightseeing. She went directly to the Broadway Tabernacle, where the American Anti-Slavery Society was meeting along with its sister organization.

It must have been exciting for Abby to meet the women about whom she had been reading so long: the Grimké sisters; Lucretia Mott, a fellow Quaker abolitionist from Philadelphia; Maria Weston Chapman, an aristocratic and beautiful Boston abolitionist; Anna Weston, Maria's sister; and many others. Even more exciting to the young school-teacher was the discovery that she had an important role to play among the women. In no time at all she was elected to a committee to help draft a statement urging other women to become active in the antislavery movement.

"An Appeal to the Women in the Nominally Free States" was the work of a committee, but it sounds very much as though Abby actually wrote it. Women could not remain aloof from the problems of slavery, the statement pointed out, since over a million women were slaves, and as many others were slaveholders. They were involved because slavery was a moral question, threatening the sanctity of the home. Even if it were wholly a political question, however, it did not follow that women should be excluded. They ought to organize antislavery societies, read antislavery literature, circulate petitions, raise money, and above all treat blacks as equals, thus getting at the prejudice in the human heart which lay at the very root of the existence of slavery.

Among other actions, the convention pledged itself to gather one million signatures for petitions opposing the annexation of Texas as a slave state and calling for the end of slavery in the District of Columbia, and set up executive committees in Boston, New York, and Philadelphia for that purpose. Back in Lynn, Abby became the driving force in the campaign for signatures. All told, the Lynn women collected some fifteen hundred. In submitting them, Abby noted that a few women might have signed their name more than once, but said she hoped that in the mass of signatures these would be overlooked.

There were more exciting things to do than circulate petitions, however. At the convention it had been decided to invite the Grimké sisters to make a tour of New England. Abby went to work making arrangements for their visit to Lynn, which occurred on June 21. In Boston and outlying towns, where the sisters had started their tour, the meetings were announced for women, though an increasing number of men attended. In Lynn the antislavery committee, largely made up of Quakers, proclaimed the meeting open to all.

This was a radical—a history-making—departure. The prejudice against women speaking before men was deep-seated and universal. The clergy reinforced it, quoting St. Paul: "But I suffer not a woman to teach, nor to usurp authority over the man, but to be in silence." According to popular opinion, a woman who exposed herself, no matter how modestly dressed, by standing up in front of an audience of men was seeking to get a response from them. Nice women would never do such a thing.

As a result of the announcement that the meeting was open, and of the sisters' growing fame, the meetinghouse was crowded beyond capacity. Some six hundred were seated, many were turned away, another hundred stood about the door, and each open window was lined with men's heads. The crush was so great that no one could circulate to take up a collection or to sign up new members for the antislavery society. The sisters spoke again the next night, and once more the following week.

Meanwhile, there were lectures to be delivered in the neighboring towns of Danvers, Salem, New Mills, and South Danvers. Abby managed these local events, in one case driving a team of horses to deliver Angelina to a lecture.

In South Danvers the sisters ran into the first incident in a long series of difficulties. The local Congregationalist minister, alarmed by the reports that they were coming, visited his fellow clergymen and persuaded them all to refuse to allow the abolitionists to lecture in a church. When the local antislavery committee hired a hall instead, the ministers used their influence to prevent notices of the meeting from being circulated, and asked members to tear them down when they were posted.

Throughout New England, in fact, the clergy were thoroughly upset. The year before, the Congregationalists had passed a resolution against itinerant agents' speaking in churches. This was aimed against the abolitionists, who created discussion and division in the churches. Now, in July, the Congregational Church sent a pastoral letter to all its clergymen, warning against strangers' preaching in churches, and deploring the practice of allowing women to participate in public meetings.

The pastoral letter aroused a storm of controversy both in the public at large and within the abolitionist movement. As a result of the letter, the Grimkés met opposition in every small town they visited. In response, Sarah Grimké began to write a series of "Letters on the Equality of the Sexes," which were published in the *New England Spectator* and reprinted in *The Liberator*. Suddenly, in every parlor, there was a new issue to discuss—the "woman question."

Within the abolitionist movement, the woman question was hotly debated. Some abolitionists, mainly members of the New England clergy, believed that women should not speak in public. Others, like John Greenleaf Whittier and Theodore Weld, while personally believing in women's rights, thought the issue of antislavery ought not to be mixed with other issues. Garrison and his immediate following, however, were delighted. They believed that the issue of women's rights and the issue of antislavery were inseparable and should be advanced at the same time. Abby, of course, agreed.

Garrison had been annoying the more conservative abolitionists for some time anyway by using the columns of *The
Liberator* to attack the church, to criticize the observance of
the Sabbath, and to publicize the views of a friend, John
Noyes, who believed that the true Christian could play no
part in any human government. Since *The Liberator* was not
the official organ of the American Anti-Slavery Society,
Garrison thought he had a perfect right to print what he
wanted in its columns. He believed in any case that the
antislavery movement could be a coalition of people with
many different points of view. It was all right for him to
believe in the rights of women; it was all right for Amos
Phelps, a Massachusetts clergyman, to disagree. All could
work together.

His critics thought not, and believed the public would be
hopelessly confused if the issues were not kept separate.
Following the pastoral letter, they issued two clerical appeals,
denouncing Garrison for his attack on the clergy and asking
that the issue of women's rights be kept out of the antislavery
crusade.

Incensed, William Lloyd Garrison responded with an
eight-column article in *The Liberator*, pointing out that
abolitionists were naturally concerned with all good causes—
peace, temperance, women's rights, home and foreign mission-
ary work—and that they could not cease to be involved in any
one in order to give more attention to the slave, as some were
suggesting, because all reforms were linked.

Abby read the editorial with enthusiasm. This was exactly
what she believed, she wrote to Garrison excitedly in the fall
of 1837. She hoped that "the time is now fully come when
thou wilt take a decided stand for all truths under the

conviction that the whole are necessary to the establishment of any single one. Those who would retreat do not understand the nature of truth, and yet how perfectly simple and easy to be understood it is to the unsophisticated child of nature." *The Liberator*, she promised, would not be rejected by many in Lynn if it should "lay the axe at the root of the tree," though it might fare worse elsewhere.

The concept of the Truth as indivisible and easily recognized by the pure in heart, stemming from Abby's Quaker upbringing, was central to her developing philosophy. She was bewildered by those who did not agree with her. They simply failed to see the whole truth, and so, obviously, they had been deceived by some evil influence. It was her job to expose error; then people would see and recognize the truth.

"I cannot tell you any news concerning myself," she wrote her sister Olive in the fall of 1837. "I pace the same old track, which is become so smooth that there is neither side nor fall, but I enjoy a good degree of comfort, notwithstanding. My variety is made up in watching the progress of moral enterprises. The temperance reform, embracing Grahamism and Abolition and Peace—and these three questions are sufficient to take up all spare time—Tis a great joy to see the world grow better in any thing—Indeed I think endeavors to improve mankind is the only object worth living for."

At twenty-six, Abby had found her real calling. She was a radical reformer.

# III

# *A Fiery Start*

IN May 1838, the second Anti-Slavery Convention of American Women was held in Philadelphia. Abby had been active in the organization throughout the year and had begun a lifelong correspondence with Maria Chapman, one of its leaders. The trip to Philadelphia was even longer and more expensive than the trip to New York, but she planned to travel with other antislavery women from New England and stay in the City of Brotherly Love with a Quaker abolitionist family, the Pennocks.

The convention was being held in Pennsylvania Hall, a new and splendid building just completed on the corner of Mulberry and Sassafrass. Leading citizens had subscribed forty thousand dollars to erect it as a public hall "wherein the principles of Liberty and Equality as well as Civil Rights can be freely discussed and the evils of slavery freely portrayed." It was to house *The Pennsylvania Freeman*, an abolitionist newspaper edited by John Greenleaf Whittier, and serve the temperance movement, as well, as a permanent headquarters.

The hall was dedicated on Monday morning, May 14, with

due ceremony, and a few of the special guests took time to poke around. The first floor contained a small auditorium, committee rooms, offices, and stores; the second floor housed a large hall with galleries. The whole was lit with modern gas, and there were ventilators in the ceiling to permit a flow of fresh air. A blue-and-white decorating scheme had been faithfully executed, with chairs lined with blue silk plush, sofas upholstered in blue damask, and the tables hung with blue silk.

If the Philadelphia reformers were proud of their new hall, however, many other Philadelphians were not equally pleased. The financial crisis of 1837, and the depression that followed it, had aroused a wave of feeling in the North against the abolitionists. Northern merchants feared the effect of the agitation on their relations with Southern businessmen. Northern laborers, many of them recent immigrants from Ireland, feared the economic competition of the free blacks. Mobs were easily incited by the fear that abolitionists believed in racial intermarriage or "amalgamation," as it was then called. The unpopular woman's issue added to the frenzy. Many unfriendly eyes had marked the building of Pennsylvania Hall, and from the moment of its dedication it was watched by angry, jeering loiterers. At first there were only a few; later there grew to be a mob.

On Monday evening, many of the abolitionists present in Philadelphia for the convention attended a wedding on Spruce Street. Angelina Grimké was marrying Theodore Weld, a notable Presbyterian minister who had made a name for himself as an antislavery lecturer in Ohio and upstate New York, converting hundreds of men and women to the antislavery cause.

Although invited, Abby could not attend. As a Quaker, Angelina was "marrying out of meeting." She would be automatically disowned by the Society of Friends, according to Quaker discipline, and any Quakers who attended the ceremony would be disowned also. Even John Greenleaf Whittier, a close friend of bride and groom, had to sit outside the door of the wedding in order to avoid censure.

Abby was becoming increasingly restless with Quaker rules, but she obeyed this one. Perhaps it was because she had mixed feelings about Angelina's marriage. The young South Carolinian was her idol; she feared that marriage might somehow interfere with her career as an antislavery lecturer. Weld was himself rather cautious on the issue of women's rights. He said he was personally committed to equality of the sexes, but he believed Garrison was wrong to mix the two issues in *The Liberator* and in the antislavery movement. Garrison for his part feared Weld's clericalism and warned Angelina against being trapped by it.

The next day, Tuesday, the convention opened. Abby had been on the arrangements committee; she entered into its sessions with enthusiasm. Early in the day, she introduced a resolution calling for the women to support the Free Produce Movement. This meant boycotting the sugar and cotton raised on Southern plantations, and using substitutes developed and sold at Free Produce stores. Quakers particularly supported the Free Produce Movement as a way of getting at the economic roots of slavery. It was not a controversial issue, and the antislavery women were glad to adopt Abby's motion.

The rest of the day passed peacefully enough, though the crowds outside of the hall increased. A few black women, members of the antislavery convention, attended the sessions, and these were particularly jeered at as they came and went from Pennsylvania Hall. Abby made a special point of getting to know Sarah Douglass, a young black antislavery lecturer. Sarah wrote to her a few days after the convention that she was glad to have met an abolitionist who had turned her back on color prejudice.

On Wednesday, May 16, the dedication ceremonies for Pennsylvania Hall were supposed to end at 3:00 P.M. The managers of the new building were just drawing a sigh of relief when an announcement was made that a public meeting, open to all, would be held in the hall that night. Since some members of the women's convention were opposed to "promiscuous" or mixed audiences, the session would be sponsored by a few individuals rather than the whole group.

Word that the "amalgamators" were holding a "promiscuous" meeting spread through the city like wildfire, and by night the hall was surrounded by a crushing mob. The alarmed managers appealed to the mayor for police protection, but His Honor was thoroughly opposed to the abolitionists and sent only a few patrolmen, all very much on the side of the crowd. Abolitionists, black and white, had to run a gantlet of jeers and catcalls on their way to the meeting. Nevertheless, there was a record turnout, with every seat taken and crowds around the doors and the windows.

The first speaker was Garrison. Perhaps stimulated by the hostility of the crowd, he gave them the cause of human rights "in good old Saxon language," as he later described it in a letter. At the end of his talk a portion of the mob surged into the hall, yelling and shouting. Part of the audience rose in some confusion and might have left had not Maria Chapman risen and with admirable self-possession spoken calmly for the next ten minutes. The crowd retreated in confusion. Next Angelina Grimké Weld came to the podium. She started quietly enough, but the mob, incensed by false rumors of "amalgamation" at her wedding, began to yell and throw brickbats. At that, her cheeks glowed, her eyes flashed, and her eloquence increased; and she "thanked God that the stupid repose of that city had at length been disturbed by the force of truth."

Esther Moore, a local Quaker, spoke briefly, followed by Lucretia Mott. The little Quaker lady explained that the meeting was not sponsored by the convention, since some of its members still disapproved of mixed audiences.

"Let us hope," she concluded piously, "that such false notions of delicacy and propriety will not long obtain in this enlightened country."

She was about to close the meeting when still another figure swept to the front of the platform. The audience gasped in surprise at the young, graceful figure, dressed in Quaker gray. From a distance, she looked like a demure young girl, though the voice that came from her lips filled the hall.

It was Abby. Moved by Angelina and Lucretia, she felt she had been impelled to her feet by the promptings of the voice within.

"I ask permission to say a few words," Abby began, glancing at the crowd. "I have never before addressed a promiscuous assembly; nor is it now the maddening rush of these voices which is the indication of a moral earthquake that calls me before you. No, not these. These pass unheeded by me. But it is the still small voice within which may not be withstood that bids me open my mouth for the dumb; that bids me plead the cause of God's poor—ay, God's poor.

"The parable of Lazarus and the rich man we may well bring home to ourselves. The North is that rich man. Now he is clothed in purple and fine linen, and fares sumptuously every day. Yonder, yonder at a little distance is the gate where lies the Lazarus of the South, full of sores and desiring to be fed from the crumbs that fall from our luxurious table. Look! See him there; even the dogs are more merciful than we. O! See him where he lies! Ought not we to raise him up, and is there no one in this Hall who sees nothing for himself to do?"

She stopped. Caught by surprise, the mob without and within had remained quiet. Her simplicity, her serenity, her audacity had taken away the breath of the hecklers. But only temporarily, for now a deep roar of anger rocked the crowd, and a rock crashed through a window and landed at Abby's feet. She looked at it for a moment with disdain, then, with a swish of her skirts, turned and went back to her seat.

The chairman banged his gavel. The evening meeting was over. From among the men and women in the front rows of the audience, a tall, rough-hewn man rose, disentangling his legs from the dainty chair. Theodore Weld rushed to the platform, to speak not to his bride but to Abby.

"You were tremendous," he congratulated her. "After this, you'll have to be an antislavery lecturer. Abby, if you don't, God will smite you."

Abby looked up into the rugged, earnest face, but heard at the same time the ugly roar of the crowd outside. Could she face all this, as Angelina had done? More important, did she have the gift? "We'll see," she said softly. "We'll see."

The noise of the crowd was becoming even louder. The abolitionists looked at each other. Then, resolutely, they began to line up two by two, a black and a white woman paired together. With Lucretia Mott near the head of the line, they left the building in close ranks, talking to each other to drown out the catcalls that surrounded them. Though there were growls from the mob, no one was hurt.

In the course of the night posters were put up all over town, urging loyal citizens to do their duty and take action against the abolitionists. Throughout the next day the crowd grew, until it was estimated at seventeen thousand. By afternoon, the managers of the hall were sufficiently alarmed to beg the antislavery women not to hold another such meeting that night. It was not in character, however, for the abolitionists to be persuaded by such appeals. Abby Kelley, for one, responded by pledging the entire New England delegation to attend. Many did likewise.

At this point the timid mayor of the city intervened, locking up the hall against further meetings, then withdrawing to City Hall and taking his policemen with him. The crowd was left unchecked. Not surprisingly, they decided to vent their rage on bricks and mortar. Rowdies burst open the doors of the hall, ransacked the offices, piled combustibles on the desks, turned on the new gas jets, and applied the torch. By 9:00 P.M. flames were shooting skyward. Fire companies, rushing to the scene, were not allowed by the mob to do more than protect the surrounding buildings. The Temple of Emancipation was offered up, in Whittier's words, as "a smoking sacrifice to the demon Slavery." By morning the new hall, the focus of so much hope, lay in ruins.

The abolitionists had felt the full force of public anger against them. And Abby Kelley had begun her new career almost literally in flames.

# IV

# *Year of Decision*

FROM fiery Philadelphia Abby went home to see her mother before proceeding to angry Boston. Here, almost the same scenario was being played. A new public building, Marlboro Hall, had just been constructed to serve as a meeting place for the abolitionists. Like Pennsylvania Hall, it was the object of public anger. The dedication, planned for the night of May 24, was almost interrupted by a mob, aroused by placards set up throughout the city. Only the prompt action of the mayor in calling up four companies of light infantry and arming them with ball cartridges, prevented violence from occurring.

Abby missed the excitement but provided her own when she arrived at Marlboro Hall the following week for the annual meeting of the New England Anti-Slavery Society. It was the first meeting since the clerical appeal had been issued. The controversy between Garrison and the clerical members of the antislavery society was in the forefront of everyone's mind, and the women's issue was considered the hottest issue in that controversy.

Early in the sessions Oliver Johnson, a young abolitionist printer, offered a resolution that women as well as men be invited to become members and participate fully in the proceedings. Amos Phelps, a clergyman strongly opposed to the women's issue, moved that the resolution be rescinded. When the majority voted against him, he and six other members asked that their names be taken from the rolls of the society and their protest printed.

Next, the convention voted to appoint a committee to send a letter, or "memorial," to all the New England religious bodies, asking them to bear their testimony against slavery. Oliver Johnson and Alanson St. Clair, a clergyman, were asked to sit on the committee. Then, in a history-making moment, Abby Kelley was also asked to serve.

Women had occasionally spoken at earlier antislavery meetings, but only after they had asked permission to do so. Abby herself had asked permission to speak at Pennsylvania Hall the week before. None before had been appointed to a committee.

Abby's head was likely in a whirl as she heard the members debating her appointment. The majority were for it, but one clergyman suggested that the memorial would be rejected if a church body knew it came from "an unscripturally woman-ruled convention," and another hinted that it would be disreputable for a woman to go off and be closeted to work on the memorial with two men.

Ought she to accept the appointment? At such times Abby felt herself ill-qualified. Though she had as good an education as any young woman of her time, she was not as well read as the men on the committee. She had no skill at writing. Her thoughts seemed to wander; she could never condense them sufficiently to get them on paper. How in the world could she help to write such an important memorial?

On the other hand, the objections being raised against her were purely on the basis of her sex. The men who argued against her appointment, she suddenly realized, had no notion of whether she was qualified or not. It was discrimination of exactly the same sort as the discrimination against the Negroes because of their black skin. And it stood in the path of herself, Abby, and of other women as well, when they tried to follow their consciences and work against slavery. A larger issue was involved, she realized, than her qualifications. Even if her reputation were stained by serving on the committee with two men, she must do it. It was her opportunity to be faithful, to serve the truth.

After debate, the convention voted by a large majority to confirm her place on the committee. When the formal meetings were over that evening, Abby went to work with her two fellow authors, and the next morning they presented their resolution. It was discussed, and Abby defended it from the floor, without bothering to ask permission to speak. The clerical abolitionists were opposed, but the Garrisonians had a majority, and the resolution, with its history-making bisexual authorship, was accepted.

This was not the end of the matter, however. All summer a controversy raged over the propriety of Abby's membership on that committee. It was the beginning of a split in the antislavery ranks over "the confounded woman question," as one exasperated abolitionist called it, and young, pretty Abby—that confounded woman!—had become its symbol.

In the back of Abby's mind for some time had been the idea of following in the footsteps of the Grimké sisters and becoming an antislavery lecturer. The heady experience of being the center of controversy made up her mind. She went back to Lynn and announced to the committee of oversight for the school that she wanted to resign. She would go home to Millbury, stay for a while with her mother, who needed companionship and care, and meanwhile prepare herself for lecturing and await divine guidance for next steps.

The Lynn Friends were reluctant to let Abby go, but she was determined, and by the end of July, they found a replacement for her. While she waited to be released, Abby wrote to friends and relations, mentioning that she was considering becoming a lecturer.

Her family reacted with consternation. The reputation of single women was jealously guarded in those days by their relatives. Propriety was a form of status. If a woman traveled around with men, or spoke on a public platform before men, people thought she was acting in a loose fashion, and might be accused of being sexually promiscuous. If Abby behaved in this fashion she would bring down shame on her entire family. Joanna Ballou, an older sister, wrote that she feared Abby was not qualified and would make herself "contemptible." Other relatives agreed. Even Abby's mother, who had taught her to follow the dictates of her own conscience, now thought she was wrong and deluded.

Support, however, came from the source she cared about most: her heroines in the antislavery struggle. There was a comforting letter from Sarah Grimké, praising her for speaking out at the Boston meetings.

"I rejoiced, dear Abby," Sarah wrote, "to hear that strength had been given thee to do thy duty there; to plead the cause of woman and in pleading our cause, the cause of the oppressed.

I am glad to find that thou were not dismayed by the opposition. What thou hast done will do more toward establishing the rights of women on this point . . . than a dozen books."

Letters of support came also from Maria Chapman, to whom Abby was becoming increasingly devoted, and from Lydia Maria Child, an antislavery novelist and journalist who wrote, "I wanted to thank you for your spirited conduct on that occasion, and I have no doubt that great good was done."

Sarah Grimké had written that she rejoiced to learn Abby was going to enjoy the "sweets and benefits" of retirement. But the sweets were short-lived. In September the Garrisonians held a convention in Boston devoted to a discussion of peace in the world and made a special point of inviting Abby. Already deeply concerned with the peace issue, she went, and promptly became once more a symbol of the woman question.

Anticipating another struggle over admitting women to membership, William Lloyd Garrison avoided the issue by a strategy. At the opening session he suggested that, since mistakes about names frequently occurred, every member should "write his or her name on a slip of paper." Some people smiled, and some frowned, but no one challenged the procedure by which women automatically became members.

Again the storm came when Abby was placed on a committee. Garrison's opponents were appalled, but said nothing. Later, however, Abby dared to call a dignified clergyman, the Reverend George Beckwith, to order. This was too much. Again, the anti-Garrison forces walked out.

The woman's issue, however, was only a sideshow to the real business of the peace convention. For several years abolitionists had been drawn increasingly to the concepts of nonresistance (today we call it nonviolence) as a means of settling conflict. Christ himself had set an example of returning good for evil, Garrison argued, and Christians should therefore never defend themselves if attacked, but have faith in the power of love to overcome the power of the sword.

An organization called the American Peace Society had for years opposed war, but it had never gone far enough, according to the radicals. A true pacifist must face the fact that all governments were built on force and administered at the point of a bayonet. If a man really had faith in nonresistance, he would never call the police, or take a case to court, or join in punishing an offender. So long as the state put people in prison, and enforced wicked laws such as those protecting slavery, a man could play no part in it, either by voting or holding office.

There was a vital connection between nonresistance and abolitionism, the Garrisonians believed. Slavery was actually enforced by the state. It would disappear as soon as men separated themselves from the wicked institution that preserved it. Force would not be needed to effect this. Rather the Prince of Peace, working through his servants, the abolitionists, would change hearts and minds all over the country, in the South as well as the North, until the wicked repented and truth reigned. It was a moral and religious crusade on which they were embarked, and government was only an impediment.

Abby believed the same thing. "The subject of Peace has of late claimed much of my attention on account of the present aspect of the abolition cause getting into the hands of politicians," she had written Maria Chapman the previous

December. "Will they not prosecute it by the sword unless the peace principles are instilled in the heart of the nation? . . . I would not abandon anti-slavery, I would engage in another enterprise which would establish abolition on an immutable basis far greater than the abolition of slavery."

Early in the Boston convention, the Reverend Henry Clarke Wright, a radical pacifist, introduced a resolution declaring that "no man, no government has the right to take the life of man, on any pretext, according to the gospel of Christ." After lively debate, the resolution was passed by a large majority, and a new organization, the New England Non-Resistance Society, was born.

Garrison, asked by the convention to prepare a Declaration of Sentiments, allowed his radicalism free range. "Never was a more 'fanatical' or 'disorganizing' instrument penned by man," he wrote his wife triumphantly. "It swept the whole surface of society, and upturned every existing institution on earth. . . . It will make a tremendous stir, not only in this country, but throughout the world."

The declaration, thus proclaimed, stated that its signers could acknowledge no allegiance to any human government and took the whole world to be their country. Not only nations, but individuals, had no right to defend themselves from attack. The nonresisters could not hold office, could not vote, could not sue a man at law or send him to prison. But while adhering to the doctrine of nonresistance and passive submission to enemies, they would "assail iniquity in high places and low."

"We expect to prevail through the foolishness of preaching," the document concluded, "striving to commend ourselves unto every man's conscience, in the sight of God."

When Garrison reported this declaration to the convention, Abby was among those who enthusiastically endorsed it. As usual, Garrison had gone to the root of the matter, she felt, and said exactly what she believed but had never before articulated. He was right: A true application of nonresistance would solve the problem of slavery, a system based on violence, and other social ills as well. She had been brought up a Quaker pacifist; now she knew that she was indeed a nonresister. The three issues—antislavery, peace, and women's rights—could not be separated. They were all of one piece to those who saw the unity of the underlying truth. The abolitionists who argued otherwise were subtly swayed by proslavery influences in the government and the church. Their errors needed to be corrected.

Stimulated afresh, Abby went back to Millbury to study and prepare herself. As the fall progressed, however, she began to have doubts, not about her beliefs but once more about her ability to express them. She had no qualifications, she felt, and lacked the knowledge of history and literature that would be necessary for her to become a spokesperson. Would she not after all make herself ridiculous? Could she stand the abuse?

"I have nothing to start upon," she wrote the Grimkés in January, "nothing to commend me to the notice or favor of any, no name, no reputation, no script, neither money in my purse. The prospect is full of trials. But what is the greatest, is the feeling of my own inability for the work. How can I make bricks without straw? I have waited thus long, hoping that I should be excused. No excuse comes. I *must* go, and yet how can I?"

Angelina wrote back a long letter. "I know by sorrowful experience what it is to feel just as thou describest, having a work to do yet not knowing how to do it, opposed by all to whom I was want to look for counsel, and bowed down under a sense of *my utter incapacity* to do what was required of my hands." She described how she had proceeded one step at a time, and urged Abby to wait for the Lord to "make a way where there now seems to be no way."

Abby worried as well about her relationship with the Society of Friends. Would her new commitment make it necessary for her to withdraw from the fellowship to which she was so strongly attached? She and her friend and fellow Quaker, William Bassett of Lynn, corresponded at length about their duty in this regard. Ought they to pull out, in protest against the Quakers' present fear of getting involved in the excitement of the antislavery cause? Or ought they to stay in, trying to move the society back to its old principles?

Abby faced a special dilemma. Thinking further about the women's rights issue, she had written to Lucretia Mott, questioning whether the Anti-Slavery Convention of American Women ought to continue to meet behind closed doors, thus themselves denying the principle for which some were struggling: the right of women to address promiscuous audiences.

"Will not the ground thou assumes oblige thee to withdraw from the Society of Friends?" Lucretia wrote back. Quakers, she reminded Abby, held their business meetings separately, though they had always worshiped together. And yet the women's meetings, "imperfect as they are, have had their use, in bringing our sex forward, exercising their talents, and preparing them for united action with men as soon as we can convince them that this is both our right and our duty." Be patient, she counseled Abby, and come to the next women's antislavery meeting, where the principle could be thrashed out.

It was one more problem for Abby to worry about. She continued to pray for light. Finally, in the early spring, she decided to sell some expensive articles of her wardrobe in answer to an urgent appeal for money for antislavery. Abby's one vanity was her wardrobe; parting with the clothes was hard for her. However, once the money was on its way to Boston, she felt better and lighter of heart.

It was shortly after this, one morning when Abby was reading from the Bible to her mother at breakfast, that she came across a passage which deeply moved her. "Not many wise men after the flesh, not many mighty, not many noble, are called, but God hath chosen the foolish things of the world to confound the wise and God hath chosen the weak things of the world to confound the things which are mighty, and base things of the world and things which are despised, and things which are not, to bring to naught things that are, that no flesh shall glory in His presence."

Abby closed the book and said to her mother, "My way is clear, a new light has broken upon me." She suddenly saw what the passage meant, she explained excitedly. In a day when the talents, the learning, the wealth, the church, and the state were all pledged to support slavery, it was necessary to go among the common people and arouse their sympathy for the victims. It was the common people who would make the difference. "I can at least cry, 'Pity the poor slave,' if I can do nothing else," she said.

Though agreeing with Abby about the evils of slavery, her mother kept hoping that it would not be necessary for Abby to become an antislavery lecturer. Abby, however, persuaded her that she had a divine calling as understood by the Society of Friends and therefore no choice in the matter.

For Abby, it was a great relief. After almost a year of turmoil, "way had opened," as the Quakers say.

# V

# *In the Eye of the Storm*

ABBY had scarcely made her momentous decision when it was time to go to New York to attend the annual meeting of the American Anti-Slavery Society. Both of the growing factions within the body looked forward to the meeting as a test of strength. At issue were many matters: Garrison's continuing sharp attacks on the clergy; his espousal of nonresistance; his opposition to all political activity. With an election coming up next year, the voting abolitionists were considering running a presidential candidate. However, the issue to divide the group most sharply was once more the confounded woman question.

Everybody who was anybody in abolitionist circles came, Abby of course included. The meetings were jammed. Garrison rose early on the first day to suggest that each person be allowed to speak only ten minutes. Even so, when the question of admitting women to membership was raised, the debate lasted all the first day and half of the second. Gerrit Smith, a wealthy philanthropist from New York State, himself a voting abolitionist, was in the chair. He said he felt sure that the convention was with him, 5 to 1, in favoring the admission of women, but when a vote was actually taken it was 180 to 140.

Amos Phelps, in a last-ditch effort, then proposed a resolution that though women were admitted to membership, it was not the intention of the society to permit them to speak, sit on committees, or fill offices. This led to a second long wrangle. Gerrit Smith pointed out that some of the member societies had already accorded women these rights. "If some prefer to send up here as their delegates your Chapmans, your Kelleys, your Barneys, have we the right to object?" he asked. "If a woman can do my work best I wish to be at liberty to select a woman."

The Phelps resolution was voted down, and Garrison, having been given the floor, yielded it to Abby Kelley. When she rose to speak, a hush fell over the audience. It was the first time since the beginning of the battle that a woman had addressed the national body. It looked as though the battle had been won. According to the record, she spoke "briefly and with great propriety." Her fellow female abolitionist, Eliza Barney, followed her. Later in the convention Abby was placed by Gerrit Smith on a committee, and still later made a brief speech from the floor. A newspaper reporter noted that while Eliza Barney could scarcely be heard, Abby's voice filled the hall.

The Garrisonians were jubilant. The problem apparently had been solved. Even though 116 members entered a formal protest, there was no split in the ranks. Abby was their new heroine.

But what of their old heroine? Little had been heard from

Angelina Grimké Weld since her final speech the night of the burning of Pennsylvania Hall, and that little was not reassuring. Coming increasingly under the influence of her husband, Theodore Weld, she had written several letters bitterly criticizing Garrison and *The Liberator*. On her way home from New York, Abby decided to stop at Fort Lee, New Jersey, where the Welds and Sarah Grimké were now living.

The visit was not reassuring. Abby had hoped that Angelina would continue to assert the rights of women despite matrimony. Instead, she found her friend deeply devoted to domesticity and very subservient to Theodore's wishes. True, Angelina was three months pregnant, and at the age of thirty-four took her condition very seriously. All three members of the little household were on a strict Graham diet of raw and natural foods and whole grains, and all took frequent plunge-baths, another new health fad of the day.

Weld himself was puzzling. After his years of fiery oratory he seemed burned out, unsure of himself. His approach to antislavery had been evangelistic. He had saved hearts and souls in the manner of a revivalist from the evils of slavery. Now, however, the new trends in the abolitionist movement disturbed him mightily. He was worried that the Garrisonians were going to produce a major schism in antislavery ranks. The mixing of other issues—nonresistance, women's rights, temperance—with the slavery issue was bound to create trouble, he felt. Garrison's increasing objections to voting were antagonizing those abolitionists—himself and Whittier among them—who believed that political action was necessary to end slavery.

"He was unsparingly severe upon us," Abby wrote to Anna Weston, a Boston friend. "Says all that Garrison, M. W.

Chapman, and all others who have adopted the will-of-a-wisp delusions of non-resistance can possibly do for the emancipation of the slave will be undermined and counteracted by their idle notions on this subject."

The Garrisonians were coming to feel that any religious observance ran counter to the true teaching of Christ. One should live out one's religion from day to day, not indulge in any outward forms. Weld, however, was still a clergyman and held family devotions daily. Abby was dismayed to observe that Angelina meekly submitted.

"Are you swallowed up and utterly annihilated in Theodore?" Abby had written to Sarah earlier in a teasing mood. Now, however, she felt it was the truth. She left Fort Lee depressed and determined never to allow such a swallowing-up to happen to her.

From Fort Lee Abby went to East Hampton, Connecticut, to the home of her older sister, Olive Darling, and Olive's husband, Newberry. She had decided to work for her room and board by helping with the housework and children while she tried a little antislavery lecturing in the Connecticut countryside. A firm Quaker still, Abby felt it would be wrong to take money for preaching. This way she could earn her keep and still follow her conscience.

She started, therefore, on a small scale by organizing a few meetings on the subject of antislavery in the immediate vicinity. They were poorly attended. The Congregational church was strong in Connecticut, and much opposed to the "excitements" of the abolitionist movement and to women lecturing. Even women who were interested dared not go to hear Abby for fear of antagonizing their husbands or their ministers.

In August Abby tried to get up a conference of women in Hartford, but that, too, was a failure. Every clergyman in the city was opposed, Abby complained, and wouldn't let the women in his congregation attend. If she were crusading for the rights of women, it appeared as though few women appreciated her efforts.

Abby, however, had an explanation. Women were like slaves, she argued, dependent upon their husbands for bread, and therefore afraid to show their true feelings. They had been educated to be led by "the lords of creation" and it was hard for them to "slip the bridle." Nevertheless, sooner or later most would awaken to the injustice of their position.

"If you can imagine a colored man's feelings, when kept at bay and held in contempt by his white brother, then can you have some faint conception of a woman's heart, when she awakes to a realizing sense of her true position, as a responsible being, and sees herself fenced in by the iron prejudice of centuries, and debarred from appearing in that position," she wrote.

She had heard about slaves who were paraded around by their masters, telling everyone how happy they were. She was not fooled by this act; neither would she be hoodwinked by the apparent coolness, even scorn, of some women. She would persist.

From Hartford, Abby went to Litchfield County in the western part of the state. Dr. Erasmus D. Hudson, an ardent abolitionist of Garrisonian persuasions, lived here, and had often urged Abby to visit. Dr. Hudson himself was away at the time, but Abby attended the meeting of the Litchfield Anti-Slavery Society, and here met several abolitionists from the nearby town of Washington, Connecticut. Two couples in particular urged her to come home with them and hold meetings in Washington. Eager to go wherever there was an opening, Abby agreed.

At Washington, Abby at first met with astonishingly courteous treatment. It was probably because one of her hosts was the sheriff and the other, the superintendent of Sabbath schools, she thought. She first spoke to a "respectable assembly of females," and though there had been talk against her in town, her message was listened to attentively.

On Sunday she attended the Congregational church with her hosts. The morning sermon was very inspiring, she thought. In the afternoon, however, the minister, the Reverend Gordon Hayes, went after Abby. He first preached a sermon on the text, "The apostles and elders came together to consider this matter," in which he asserted the right of church officials to make decisions for the congregation. He then announced that he had been asked to read aloud a notice of a meeting in which a woman was expected to address a mixed assembly.

This he could not do without stating that he believed it to be wrong, he said. The woman in question was a nonresistant, advocating the principles which would open the jails, prevent the collection of taxes, and permit the rule of violence. St. Paul had taught that it was a sin and a shame for a woman to speak in church. And did they not have a clear warning from the Old Testament? He read from Revelation, "I have a few things against thee because thou sufferest that woman, Jezebel, which calleth herself a prophetess, to teach and seduce my servants to commit fornication." He urged members of the congregation to ask themselves if a woman who traveled alone by night and by day, sometimes with a pack of men, was a proper person to speak to them. Would they all please stay after the service, and express their opinion on the propriety of the woman in question speaking to mixed audiences?

No one looked at Abby. Abby herself stared straight ahead. Meekly the congregation approved the resolution against female lecturers. The service ended, and the people filed out. Though Abby was standing near the door, no one spoke to her.

Abby was crushed. The insinuation that she was sexually lax was one which cut her so deeply she could think of no rejoinder. She could, however, protest. As the parson walked out she went up to him and said, "Gordon Hayes, you have said things most injurious to my character. I hope God will forgive you."

Perhaps the people of Washington repented their intolerance, or perhaps they were curious. At any rate, Abby spoke to a large mixed audience that very night, and again Tuesday. "The slanders had no other effect than to increase her faith and animate her zeal," a local observer wrote enthusiastically to *The Liberator*.

It was not true, however. Underneath, Abby was deeply hurt and shaken. The fears expressed by friends and relations seemed to have been justified. Her reputation was ruined, and Abby cared. Thereafter she refused to travel without a chaperone. When she told her good friend Elizabeth Buffum Chace about these charges, tears always came to her eyes. Years later, when as an old woman she wrote her memoirs, the one incident she recalled the most vividly—though not quite accurately—was the time she was first called Jezebel.

Despite the hurt, however, Abby went on. Throughout the

fall and winter of 1839 and the early spring of 1840, she continued to make East Hampton her headquarters and to plow the stubborn field of Connecticut. In March she was able to write Garrison that she had held sixty-five meetings, mainly with Baptists, Congregationalists, and Methodists; that she had been opposed by only two antislavery ministers; and that she was making headway on the woman question. "Of course there is at first a strong prejudice against women's talking in company, if the company shall happen to be called a meeting, but it soon vanishes, for they immediately discern the fact that it is no new thing for women to talk; it is a very commonplace affair, and not hideous in the least."

If women could talk in the parlor, then why not in a public hall? Abby could get no satisfactory answer. One learned doctor of divinity merely said that public opinion was against it. In an article which she wrote for the Hartford *Observer*, Abby asked, "Will Sir Public Opinion have the kindness to define the exact boundary between a large and a small number, and show how it is sinful to speak in orderly meetings, when at the same time it is no sin to speak in disorderly ones?"

Women ought to be allowed to use the same ways and means to reform the world as men, she argued in the same article, because such means are strictly moral, and God asked of every human being, male or female, black or white, that he use his powers to the advancement of the human race. "If we can but obtain the pure waters of truth, why should we be so scrupulous about the form of the vessel through which we receive it?"

Abby had planned the article as the first of a series, but so many readers were offended that the editor canceled the rest. Sir Public Opinion was still strong.

As May 1840 approached, excitement mounted throughout the antislavery movement. The voting abolitionists had held a series of meetings and organized a third party, the Liberty party, to run James Birney for President and Thomas Earle for Vice President in the November elections. A group of clergymen who had withdrawn from the Massachusetts Anti-Slavery Society to form a new organization had been hard at work during the winter and spring, lining up forces to combat Garrison at the American Anti-Slavery Society's anniversary meetings. After simmering for several years, the bitter controversy between abolitionists was about to come to a boil.

Both sides did what they could to bring as many delegates as possible to the meetings. The anti-Garrison forces even persuaded a large group of women to come, prepared to vote against women's rights. The Garrisonians chartered a special steamboat to sail from Providence to New York for the event and convinced the management to relax the Jim Crow rules so that black and white delegates could ride together. To bring the New England abolitionists to Providence, two extra trains were chartered.

"There were about 450 antislavery men and women among us of whom about 400 were from Massachusetts," Garrison wrote, in describing the event. (Probably another 100 went by other routes.) "There was never such a mass of 'ultraism' afloat in one boat, since the first victim was stolen from the fire-smitten and blood-red soil of Africa."

The papers were full of the news of the impending event, and by the time the Garrison party reached New York there was a mob waiting to storm the Graham house, where they had taken lodgings, and follow them through the streets, taunting them and throwing stones.

Once inside the Fourth Free Church, where the annual meeting was to be held, the scene was hardly less stormy. Over one thousand delegates were present and Francis Jackson, the vice president, had to shout to make himself heard.

Abby of course was there, having come with the Massachusetts delegation. All eyes were on her. She was the woman who had caused the first split in the abolition movement. Would she play the same role at this climactic hour?

Jackson had scarcely called the meeting to order before he appointed a business committee. The names he rolled off represented a fair cross-section of the movement. Amos Phelps, Ichabod Codding, and Lewis Tappan were clearly with the New Organization forces; Garrison and Charles C. Burleigh with the Old. But then Jackson added, "Miss Abby Kelley of Massachusetts," and pandemonium filled the hall. Men rose to speak, to present resolutions, to shout defiance. Cries of "Order, order" came from the chair. Abby herself attempted to speak on behalf of the rights of women. "I rise because I am not a slave," she shouted.

Debate continued for some time. Finally a vote was taken: 451 to unseat Abby, 557 in her favor. The hall broke into a storm of clapping and hissing, until Garrison asked for the clapping to stop. Then a large group of abolitionists, including many of those who had organized the movement in New York State, withdrew to form a new organization, the American and Foreign Anti-Slavery Society. The antislavery movement was now formally split into two organizations, called the Old and the New. As the first woman to demand her right to speak in public, Abby was the immediate cause.

Garrison and his friends seemed to welcome the split. It would permit them to pursue antislavery without compromises. More moderate abolitionists, however, were appalled at the spectacle of reformers fighting among themselves. Whittier wrote to a friend that he was "off women" as a result of Abby's role in "blowing up the Anti-Slavery Society. . . . I suppose thee will say it is all right, but it seems to me rather out of the way to say the least of it," he commented tartly.

Abby thought it was a shame too. "The abolitionists are busy abolishing antislavery," she remarked to a friend.

The split widened still further at the World Anti-Slavery Convention held in London, in June. Both the Pennsylvania and the Massachusetts delegations included several women, Lucretia Mott among them. When they arrived in London they were told that they would not be admitted as delegates but could watch the proceedings from the gallery. A long argument ensued. The enemies of both Garrison and Lucretia had written ahead to warn the British against them, and Garrison himself was delayed at sea. The resolution offered by the American abolitionist Wendell Phillips to admit women was voted down by a large majority, and Lucretia and her friends consigned to the gallery.

Abby Kelly's name had been on the original list of delegates from Massachusetts, but she had chosen instead to continue her work in Connecticut. Nevertheless, her spirit was very much present. "Imagine the indignation of such a woman as Abby Kelley," Elizabeth Cady Stanton, a young bride attending the conference with her husband, exclaimed. Though she was not herself a delegate, she too was moved with indignation. She sought out Lucretia Mott, and the two began conversations which were to result eight years later in the first women's rights convention, held in Seneca Falls.

By acting on her belief that women had a right to be heard, Abby had set the spark that flamed in time into the women's rights movement.

# VI

# Summer of Abuse

THE newspapers throughout the country played up Abby's role in splitting the American Anti-Slavery Society. By the time she returned to Connecticut, she was notorious. When her name was mentioned, people not only thought about women's rights, they also associated her in their minds with every radical idea then current. They knew she was opposed to both church and state; they imagined she might also believe in free love, or "no-marriage-perfectionism" as it was then called.

The no-marriage ideas had been advanced by Frances Wright, a young Scots radical who had come to the United States in the 1820s and also spoken to mixed audiences. Since Angelina Grimké had also lectured to "promiscuous" assemblies, Abby was not the first, but the third, woman in the United States to do this. Nevertheless, she seemed to be the target of more abuse than her predecessors.

Perhaps it was because she was pretty, and people in this repressed age felt there was something lewd about a pretty woman lecturing in public. Or perhaps it was because, with her sharp tongue and fiery nature, she put her critics in their place. Whatever the reason, she took on herself the full weight of the anger that organized society felt for the radical idea that women might have the same rights as men. The women of the day came to admire her, and to regard her as a martyr.

Abby's tumultuous Connecticut summer began with her attendance at the Connecticut Anti-Slavery Society's annual meeting in Saunders Hall in New Haven, to which she went directly from New York. The antislavery movement in Connecticut was dominated by the clergy and was therefore heavily committed to the New Organization. The battle that had been won in New York had to be fought all over again.

Once more, the question of admitting women to the full rights of membership was debated. When Abby, accustomed now to asserting herself, rose to speak on the subject, the chairman, the Reverend H. G. Ludlow, ruled her out of order. This ruling was overriden by voice vote. Abby proceeded with her speech. Antislavery societies were supposed to be nonsectarian, she argued, but if they ruled against women they ruled against one sect, the Quakers, who believed women had a right to speak in public.

"Abby Kelley is a Quakeress, about 25 years, distinguished by her effrontery in practically asserting the right of her sex to an equal place with men," a reporter from the New Haven *Record* wrote. "The woman . . . proceeded with her speech with the most perfect self-possession."

When at last she was through, the chairman announced that he would resign. "The scene we have just witnessed convinces me more than ever that it is dangerous to allow women to have a voice in public deliberations," he declared.

"Their influence is too powerful, yet not by the power of their arguments, but by the fascination of their looks and the sorcery of their tongues, by taking advantage of the gallantry of men, they would in all cases carry the day, whether their cause was right or wrong.

"I had enough of woman control in the nursery. Now I am a man, I will not submit to it, . . . I will not sit in a meeting where women are allowed to speak and vote," the chairman concluded and, seizing his hat, rushed out of the hall in undignified haste.

Another chairman, Francis Perkins, was appointed, and the debate continued. Abby at length rose to speak.

"Sit down—take your seat, madam," the chairman ordered her.

"I am bound in duty to God and man to speak, and the constitution of the Society gives me the right," Abby answered.

"I hope Miss Kelley and the other women will learn decency and modesty by and by, and not presume to speak and vote with men," another clergyman shouted.

The debate continued to rage, but the Garrisonians were outnumbered and the ruling against Abby was sustained. They did not, however, give up easily.

As the crowd broke up in some confusion, a friend of Abby's jumped on a chair and announced that Abby would speak that very afternoon in a public hall in New Haven.

The account of this meeting in the New Haven *Record* spread Abby's fame still further. Wherever she went to lecture, crowds came to see this new curiosity, a forward woman. Ministers warned their congregations against her, and parents feared that she would contaminate the morals of their

children. Teenage boys and girls were captivated by her spirit
of rebellion and wrote her letters, sometimes without the
knowledge of their elders.

"Thou art accused (like another Socrates) of introducing
new Gods; of corrupting the minds of the young; enticing
them from the path of rectitude; beguiling them from the
church, and so perverting their understandings by thy
sophistry, as to lead them to discard all religion," one young
girl called Sarah wrote to her. "Well may our elders tremble,
the temple they have erected to their God sectarianism quivers
and totters at its very base."

Several times there were ugly scenes. In South Cornwall, a
small Connecticut town, a mob formed outside of one of
Abby's meetings and threw rotten eggs and "the contents of
outhouses" in through the windows. The next night a
military company marched up and down outside another of
her meetings, trying to drown out the sound of her voice with
constant drumming and fifing.

In a neighboring town, Cornwall Bridge, it was even worse.
People had just settled down to an evening meeting in a
schoolhouse to hear Abby when a drunken man burst in with
a large club in his hand shouting, "Where is the nigger bitch
that is going to lecture here this evening? Where is she? Tell
me where is she?"

Receiving no answer, the drunkard began to stride up and
down the aisles, smashing the glass-encased candles with his
club. Abby, pale and trembling, was hurried out the back, but
several members of the audience received glancing blows. The
hall was hurriedly emptied, just as more armed men joined the
original bigot.

Undaunted, Abby went ahead with plans for a meeting the

next afternoon at the Methodist church, but once more the bully and his armed friends showed up. The local police, although present, took no action, and the abolitionists finally adjourned to a private home amid catcalls and insults. Here Abby spoke serenely to a large audience containing several of the men who had threatened her the night before.

Violent scenes like these seemed to bring out a vein of iron in Abby. Cold rejection she always found much more difficult to bear. Arriving in Norwalk, Connecticut, one Friday, she presented herself at the home of a doctor who had been described to her as a friend of the Garrisonians. Her host, however, was out of town, and his wife did not share his views. The lady received Abby coldly, and barely spoke to her in the course of the weekend. Several leading citizens of the town came to call but promised her no help, and on Saturday, a well-dressed gentleman walked in off the street and shook his fist in her face. No one in the household intervened.

Chilled by the hostility in the household, Abby asked a young medical student staying there if she could get a room in a local hotel but was told that she was regarded as a "vile woman" and would not be received. There was no way to get to the next town until Monday, and Abby ended by sitting in her room, waiting for the hours to pass. "Words cannot describe the spiritual anguish of that long day and night," she wrote. "A rap at my door announced dinner, another supper, and then breakfast. I could not eat in that house."

Finally, on Monday morning, a lukewarm abolitionist drove her to the nearby town of Canaan, to the home of a Quaker farmer and his wife. They received Abby with kindness and warmth, gave her a room and a meal, and invited her to make herself at home. Abby was overjoyed by their kindness. "I went into the orchard, back of the house, and ran about like a colt let loose," she reported. "I climbed the trees, and sang with the birds. I hopped, skipped, and danced. Such ecstasy comes but rarely. When called to dinner, I could eat. A farmer's boiled pot had never had such flavor as that."

Abby stayed with the Quaker couple and held several successful meetings in Canaan. It must have restored temporarily her tottering faith in her fellow Quakers, and her fellow human beings as well. In the next town, however, she was in trouble again. She had barely commenced a meeting in the town hall when the church bell began to peal vigorously, horns hooted, tin pans were banged. When Abby asked if the noise could be stopped, she was told that the boys might as well have their sport. She dismissed the meeting and went home to rest up for another round.

Frequently during this terrible summer, money was a problem. Abby was still accepting no help from the American Anti-Slavery Society, and was too busy lecturing to take time to earn her keep. At her meetings, she did not ask for contributions for herself, but several times, just as she was down to a few coins, a basket was passed, or a letter arrived in the mail containing a five-dollar bill. Her clothes grew worn, and she lost weight, but she survived. The Bostonians thought her ordeal improved her: She was more accomplished, more graceful, more charming as a result.

In October the Boston Female Anti-Slavery Society held its antislavery meeting. Abby was the principal speaker. She was now so famous that the committee for arrangements was eager to advertise her mere presence in order to draw a crowd, and her speech was enthusiastically reported in the antislavery press.

"By the way, Abby is taking the field like a lion," one abolitionist wrote another. "What a speech in *The Liberator* and how superbly reported."

The speech in question was Abby's best to date. She began by saying that she had no gift "to string together brilliant sentences or beautiful words." Her mission was among the hills and hamlets, propounding simple truths to the unsophisticated. She always reminded her country audiences that the United States had been founded sixty years ago on the basis of liberty for all. Yet by denying liberty to the two and a half million fellow humans who were the slaves, the new nation had imperiled the liberties of all.

"We were not aware that the mere existence of slavery in any section of our land would endanger the liberties of the whole; well it is, then, that we have learned that we demolished the cornerstone of our own freedom, when we consented that man should be enslaved at all. All the great family of mankind are bound up in one bundle. Rights are the same for one and all; and when we aim a blow at our neighbor's rights, our own rights are by the same blow destroyed."

Many of the women in this hall had thought they were free, Abby reminded them, until they and their male colleagues began to agitate for the end of slavery. Then they found out exactly how free they were. "You were free to be mobbed—free to be slandered and misrepresented to any amount—free to be driven from your place of meeting by five thousand of the most respectable and gentlemanly of your friends, called together by public advertisements for the express purpose. Our country saw then what their liberty amounted to—liberty to speak what slavery should dictate.

Men were awakened then to a realizing sense of their freedom.

"Free were they? Yes! Free to the tar caldron and the feather bag! Free to have a bonfire made of their furniture before their own doors in the open street! Free to be whipped and imprisoned! Free to be shot down! A great freedom indeed was this."

In her ringing conclusion, Abby urged all to open themselves to sympathy for the slave, to act upon that sympathy, before it dried up within them, and not to expect any help from the rich and the mighty. "For one, I rejoice to be identified with the despised people of color," she told her Boston audience. "If they are despised, so ought we their advocates to be. It is a poor policy, for it is a wicked policy which would make two bands of us. We hear about retaining our influence by not being identified with them. But what was the example of our Saviour? The publicans and the sinners were his associates—the poor and the despised!"

Though the women applauded Abby enthusiastically, most of them knew in their heart of hearts they could never follow her example. She had literally identified herself with the slaves, and had drawn down upon herself the wrath of a good part of the nation. Preachers thundered at her from the pulpit, editors lampooned her in the papers. Crowds molested her. The epithet *Jezebel* followed her from town to town. To the antislavery women she was more a Joan of Arc. Jezebel or Joan of Arc, she was unique, a courageous woman, a household name.

"If I were one of those Abby Kelley women I would have told them my views, and shaken dust from their eyes," one woman told another.

# VII

# *The Comeouters*

THE ferocity with which the clergy in Connecticut attacked her further convinced Abby Kelley that the church itself was an apologist for slavery. By failing to support antislavery efforts, local ministers were actually helping slave-owners keep their grip on the nation, she believed. In this way the Christian church was really condoning all the evils of slavery: the separation of family, the forced prostitution of black women to their white masters, the brutal floggings and even death of slaves. It had become guilty of these very sins itself. It was an evil institution, and the only thing a true Christian could do was separate herself from it.

In November, Abby attended a convention at the Chardon Street Chapel in Boston called by a group of Garrisonians to discuss the present state of the church. Among other issues debated was the practice of keeping Sunday, or the Sabbath, separate and holy. Christianity should be expressed throughout people's lives, the convention members argued, not just on special occasions. Though many clergymen attended the meetings and presented differing points of view, most of the church of New England reacted violently against the convention, and Garrison was accused of leading an infidel group. Abby regarded herself as no infidel, and was freshly angered at the church.

In many ways the Garrisonians were behaving like the early Quakers: interrupting church services, refusing to go along with empty ceremonies, admitting women to full equality. Nevertheless Abby found the contemporary Society of Friends more and more disappointing; in their zeal to keep out of the controversy of the antislavery movement, "to keep in the quiet," they were actually hurting the very cause they had once espoused. Her good friend William Bassett had been disowned by the Lynn Friends for his antislavery activities. Even Lucretia Mott, she feared, had been too timid in London about asserting women's rights for fear of further antagonizing the Society of Friends.

Early in 1841 Abby wrote a letter to *The Liberator* criticizing New England Yearly Meeting, to which she belonged, for closing its meetinghouses to antislavery lecturers. Getting no answer from the Yearly Meeting, she decided later in the spring to take the step she had long contemplated. Though she knew it would hurt her mother and many of her good friends and relations, she felt she could no longer be a member of the Society of Friends. She therefore addressed a letter to Uxbridge Meeting announcing her wish to "come out and be separate" from its fellowship.

The plain speech and plain dress, once adopted by the Quakers to get away from meaningless sophistication, had themselves become empty forms, she argued in her letter. The Quakers no longer played an active role in the antislavery or nonresistance movements, and thus had turned their backs on their own historic testimonies. In fact, having a worldwide reputation as abolitionists, the Quakers were making things much worse by espousing all the arguments advanced by the slaveholders, although they did it in the name of "keeping in the quiet."

The Uxbridge Meeting ignored the letter, but in the summer of 1841 began disownment proceedings against Abby. A committee of the women's meeting was appointed to "have an opportunity" with her. Abby refused to see them. The meeting then acknowledged that perhaps an interview was unnecessary, since Abby had made her views known elsewhere. In October she was formally disowned.

Abby, however, intended to disown the Quakers, not have them disown her. She managed to have the last word publicly by arranging for Garrison to publish her letter in *The Liberator*, also in October.

"To say that Friends must wait until the Lord opens the way is blasphemy," she wrote Garrison. "He never shut the way."

To withdraw publicly from a proslavery church was a favorite technique of the Garrisonians. The idea came from an earlier mystical movement with its origins in Cape Cod, involving the separation of the true Christian from the church. It was called "Cape Cod Comeouterism" or simply "comeouterism." In her letters during the summer of 1841, Abby compared notes with other friends who had made the same step. The antislavery papers were full of such letters.

A more spectacular form of comeouterism was being practiced in New England at this time. A group of young men, all antislavery radicals, were interrupting church services in order to preach the antislavery gospel. Not surprisingly, this behavior made the preacher and the congregation very angry, and the comeouters were hustled, dragged, and pushed out of the church. None of them resisted this treatment, for they were nonresisters to a man. They believed in returning good for evil, and using spiritual, not physical, weapons. Instead they went limp, allowed themselves to be dragged out, and then, as soon as they were able, came back in again. Soon they had stirred up a hornet's nest of excitement all over New England.

The most radical of all the radical comeouters was a man called Stephen Symonds Foster, a rugged New Hampshire man with a fierce look and gentle blue eyes. Foster was born in 1809, in Canterbury, the ninth child in a family of twelve. His father, Asa, had joined the Revolutionary Army at the age of thirteen and fought under General Arnold in Saratoga. For this service he was offered bounty, but having come to believe that war was wrong, he refused to accept it. Instead, he managed to scrape a living out of the hard soil of New Hampshire for his growing family.

Coming from this rugged environment, Stephen was a hardworking, earnest young man. Until he was twenty-two he earned his living as a carpenter and builder. He then decided to study for the ministry and went to Dartmouth College. Soon, however, he was in trouble, for when it was his turn to serve in the militia, he refused on conscientious grounds, because of his opposition to war, and was placed in the Haverhill jail. Instead of feeling sorry for himself, he befriended the other inmates, many of whom were there for debt rather than crime, and all of whom suffered from the filthy conditions of the jail. An angry letter from Stephen to the state authorities resulted in a cleanup of the jail, a reform of New Hampshire's prison system, and the end of imprisonment for debt. In his early twenties he was already an effective reformer.

From Dartmouth Stephen went to Union Theological Seminary to prepare further for the ministry. Once more, however, his antiwar stand led to difficulties. When he tried to hold an antiwar prayer meeting and the faculty refused to allow him to use a lecture room, Stephen decided to withdraw and devote his life to reform.

Shortly after he left the seminary, Stephen met Parker Pillsbury, a radical abolitionist and kindred spirit. Together the two of them began to speak out in local meetings and churches against slavery, until they had evolved the techniques of breaking up services by passive resistance.

In the fall of 1841, for example, Stephen went into old North Church, the first Congregational church in Concord, New Hampshire. Just as the minister was about to begin his sermon, Stephen stood up and began to speak. The startled pastor tried to interrupt, but Foster kept going until three members of the congregation took him by the arms and led him out the door. In ten minutes he was back, again preaching. The minister ordered the choir to drown him out, but Foster could outshout them. Finally, he was escorted out again, more violently. When he returned once more to disturb the afternoon session, some members of the congregation lost their tempers, dragged him down the aisle, kicked him, and threw him down a pair of stairs. Stephen was wearing an old top hat, which was badly battered in the process. It became a symbol to him of the battle in which he was now engaged.

After spending two weeks in bed recuperating from his

injuries, Stephen pleaded his own cause before the judge but was declared guilty of disturbing the peace and ordered to pay five dollars. He had no such sum, but his friends managed to raise the money, a few coins at a time.

The beatings and the jailings continued. In 1842 he wrote to a friend:

> I am now laid on the shelf for the present, perhaps for the winter. Possibly even for a longer period. Indeed, when I dare to look on my shattered form I sometimes think prisons will be needed for me but a little longer. Within the last fifteen months four times have they opened their dismal cells for my reception.
>
> Twenty-four times have my countrymen dragged me from their temples of worship, and twice have they thrown me with great violence from the second story of their buildings, careless of the consequences. Once in a Baptist meetinghouse they gave me an evangelical kick in the side, which left me for weeks an invalid. Times out of memory have they broken up my meetings with violence, and hunted me with brickbats and bad eggs. Once they have indicted me for assault and battery. Once in the name of outraged justice, have they attempted to put me in irons. Twice have they punished me with fines for preaching the gospel, and once in a mob of two thousand people have they deliberately attempted to murder me. . . . Still, I would not complain, though death should be close on my track. My lot is easy compared with that of those for whom I labor.

It was in the summer of 1841, just after Abby had resigned

from Uxbridge Meeting, that the two of them met on the antislavery lecture trail in New Hampshire. Stephen was thirty-two, Abby thirty. Both had set aside thoughts of romance and marriage for the sake of the cause. Both were vital, exciting, extreme in their views. It was natural that they were almost immediately drawn to each other. Stephen first saw her, he wrote many years later, "as a vigorous, animated, bounding creature." Abby did not record her first impressions, but in September she was defending Stephen's tactics in a letter in *The Liberator.*

Stephen had come to Millbury in the course of the summer and had conducted a series of lectures attacking the churches, which he called "man-stealing, woman-whipping, adulterous, and murderous."

"He was harassed, abused, and threatened with a pistol but he persisted until he made Millbury an antislavery town," Abby wrote enthusiastically. His discourse is thrilling, she also observed.

Stephen needed defense if he was to be accepted by the Boston clique, the little group surrounding Garrison who ruled the American Anti-Slavery Society. Maria Chapman, Wendell Phillips, and others found Stephen's extremism distasteful and thought his methods were more apt to hurt than to help.

Stephen's virulent attack on the church was sometimes the source of embarrassment. Having once wanted to be a minister, Stephen went after the clergy with all the anger of a rejected lover. Churches were brothels, since they supported slavery, which supported prostitution. They were dens of thieves, full of adulterers and murderers, by the same logic. Stephen always carried his point to extremes. If a man did not agree with his exact antislavery views, he argued that that man was in reality a supporter of slavery.

Abby rejoiced in Stephen's attack on the clergy, for she herself was continuing her running battle with them. In a Connecticut antislavery meeting Ichabod Codding, the clergyman prominent in the New Organization, implied that she was a loose, evil woman. "She repeatedly allowed herself to be placed on committees with men," he charged, and "in 1839 she was appointed to a committee with two men, one married, the other unmarried and they went off together in an upper loft to examine the books of the Society."

Once more, Abby was stung. In a letter in the new publication the *National Anti-Slavery Standard*, Abby asked Mr. Codding publicly whether he would have been any happier if she had spoken to two married men.

With brief trips home to visit her ailing mother, Abby continued to lecture against slavery in Connecticut and in New Hampshire. Her notoriety continued, and the opposition against her grew increasingly violent. In Norwich, Connecticut, all the churches were closed to her and it was publicly stated that most good citizens would rather be seen walking down the streets with "a nigger" as with Abby Kelley. "I am proud to be identified with the despised people of color," Abby wrote passionately, repeating an earlier theme. "I thank the God of the poor that I was accounted worthy of such an honor."

One day Abby preached in a Baptist church in Fitchburg, Connecticut, against the relationship between slavery and religion. Just as she was getting well started, a slaveholder with fifteen followers, all holding pistols, burst in the nave. The audience was frightened. Several people started to rise.

Abby, however, managed to keep going without skipping a word. Robbed of the sensation he expected to create, the slaveholder did not quite know what to do next. He wavered and began to listen to the sermon. His followers did not know where to turn, and one by one withdrew. Finally, the slaveholder sat down and listened to Abby, as though spellbound.

"The power of the Lord restored the slaveholder to his senses," an observer wrote enthusiastically.

In the fall of 1841 Abby moved her headquarters to Rhode Island, where there was a strong popular move for a new state constitution, led by a man named Thomas Dorr. According to the old constitution, suffrage was limited to landholders and their oldest sons. This disenfranchised half the adult males. Working-class people in the cities had no voice in government. On the other hand, the Dorr Constitution limited suffrage to white males. Abby and her friends objected on principle, and Abby spoke publicly against it.

As a result, she again reaped a whirlwind. Editors attacked her, clergymen preached against her, the doors of most churches were closed. She was accused again of corrupting the minds of youth. Even the Free Will Baptists, an antislavery sect, refused to sponsor a meeting. In the white heat of anger, she wrote that they "drank the blood of the slave second-handed," since they received communion from the altar of the same church that elsewhere dispensed it to slaveholders.

This charge, published in the *National Anti-Slavery Standard*, brought an angry response from the Free Will Baptists. Lydia Maria Child, editor of the *Standard*, apologized for Abby. "Let them not forget in extenuation that she is a most laborious, self-sacrificing, and efficient friend of the enslaved, let them remember she was persecuted by falsehood and abuse from all quarters and followed by the hissing and the pelting of a mob," she explained.

Huge mobs did in fact collect in Newport and throughout Rhode Island in the last days of the 1841 campaign to protest Abby's activities. One day a mob of about one thousand followed Abby and her companion from the lecture hall to her rooming house, shrieking insults and pelting the two women with decayed apples, rotten eggs, and offal. Abby managed as usual to remain calm under fire. She encouraged her trembling comrade onward, step by step. Miraculously, they reached their rooms without being hurt.

Abby had a happy faculty for quickly forgetting this sort of abuse. It was probably a psychological shield that guarded her from shock and hurt, but she had another explanation: "Such scenes, a few days after their occurrence, are to me like troubled dreams," she wrote. "They leave no clear impression, from the fact, I suppose, that I cannot persuade myself that the people are really as wicked as to be guilty of such atrocities."

Some things, however, got through her guard and rankled inside her. Then she remembered them for years afterwards. When an editor accused her of lewdness because she stood up in a mixed audience and waved her arms, without so much as a shawl around her shoulders, her feelings were deeply wounded.

The Dorr Constitution was defeated, thanks in part to the abolitionists. As soon as the campaign was over, Abby returned to Millbury to look after her ailing mother. Mrs. Kelley had been her responsibility ever since Wing Kelley's death. Abby managed her mother's finances, handled the property, and saw to it that Diana had company whenever Abby had to be away lecturing. The older sisters were married and lived at a distance. Lucy came and went without much sense of responsibility, Abby thought. Albert was married and raising a rapidly increasing family. Everyone looked to Abby to manage.

Now the managing was sad, for Mrs. Kelley, who had had a bad cough for several years, was failing rapidly. On February 14, 1842, she died. Abby grieved, arranged for the funeral, and stayed on to make plans for settling the estate. There was no question in Abby's mind where her share of the meager inheritance would go. The American Anti-Slavery Society needed every penny she could scrape up for it.

# VIII

# *New Fields to Conquer*

As early as the spring of 1840, Abby began to receive urgent invitations to lecture against slavery in New York State. The Liberty party, organized to run candidates in the election of 1840, was converting all the antislavery forces in the state to its cause. This was a blow to Garrison's Old Organization and a victory for New Organization forces. Garrison needed a spellbinder like Abby to take the field.

The Garrisonians' opposition to the Liberty party sounded like intermovement rivalry to outsiders and seemed quite incomprehensible. Radicals like Abby, however, really believed that engaging in politics was a positive evil. It took people's energies away from the real struggle, which was to change minds and hearts, North and South. It gave legitimacy to the corrupt state, and settled for mere reform, when what was needed was revolution.

By the summer of 1842, Abby was ready to leave New England and try the new territory. It was quite a change. In

Connecticut and Rhode Island she had known the persecution of the mobs and the ridicule of the clergy, but few physical hardships. New England was long settled, small towns were only a few miles apart, and houses were snug and comfortable.

Western New York, however, was closer to the frontier. Here, and in Ohio and Indiana, which she visited later, Abby came into territory where homes were widely scattered and often crude, roads impassable in the muddy season. She learned to endure the hardships of bumping along corduroy roadbeds by day, and sleeping at night wherever she could get a bed. Sometimes she found herself in the same room as a man and his wife. Often the whole family shared a single washbowl and ate out of a single fryingpan. Abby tried not to fuss, but she did like a pan of water of her very own, and she sometimes asked for an egg or a potato rather than share the greasy food. Bedbugs bothered her. She caught cold easily and was plagued with colds and sore throats and fevers as she traveled about in open cutters in the icy winter.

She was not only uncomfortable and often sick; she was frequently down to her last few cents. She continued to refuse to accept pay for her services, and when there was an opportunity to raise money she asked people to give to the American Anti-Slavery Society, or to buy subscriptions to the *National Anti-Slavery Standard*, rather than to pay for the expenses of the meeting.

She survived from hand to mouth, going from one hospitable antislavery family to another, and looking for free rides from town to town. Often she approached a new village with only a slender lead. Someone had given her the name of a man or a woman supposed to be active in the cause. If the person turned out to be out of town, or cool to women lecturers, she had to hunt up housing in a public house and pay for it out of her own purse.

Once she found herself lodging in a new town, her work had only just begun. Then it was time to set up meetings, arrange for the use of a public house, notify the newspapers, have notices posted. No matter how sick or tired she was, these things must be attended to immediately.

In the cities she fared a little better. Albany, the capital of New York State, had a population of 33,000 and supported twenty-five churches. Rochester and Buffalo had both grown from frontier villages to bustling cities of 20,000 each, due to the recently built Erie Canal. In each of these metropolitan areas there were local abolitionists to give her some hospitality and some aid.

She began her work in New York State in July and moved slowly across the state. The reporter who had been assigned by the Albany *Tocsin* to cover her speeches in that city expected a roaring lion of a woman. Instead he found her modest, retiring, almost diffident, "a plain country girl." Nevertheless, rowdies popped small beer bottles and dashed paving stones at the windows during her speech. It looked very much as though New York were going to be as exciting as Connecticut.

In Albany, Abby stayed with the Motts, an abolitionist family. After she had left, Abigail Mott wrote to Abby suggesting that she rest, watch her health, and be careful of her reputation. "*Caution* as you are travelling with Fred Douglas (sic). I advise you to be careful who hears your regrets you are not a colored woman," Abby Mott warned in a cramped postscript.

Frederick Douglass, an escaped slave, was an antislavery lecturer also that summer in western New York. Later, in Utica, Abby was criticized for walking the streets with Charles Remond, another black antislavery agent. The rumor persisted that Abby was a "nigger lover" and slept with black men. "We are sometimes called a travelling seraglio," she complained angrily. Most of the time she took with her an old Quaker woman as traveling companion, but even Margaret Prior's sober bonnet and honest face didn't keep the rumors down.

As she traveled westward, following the string of villages along the Erie Canal, Abby found she had more than her reputation to worry about. She had come to New York confident in her ability to win converts to her side by pointing out the inequities of church and state. Both helped to support slavery, either directly or indirectly. Only by being wholly separate from them could the true Christian serve the true cause of antislavery.

The Liberty party had already gained so much strength, however, that her arguments did not work. Some people scarcely seemed to know what she was talking about. Others, won over to antislavery by her arguments, were easily influenced a day or so later by Liberty party organizers.

Abby got off to a bad start by announcing a few days after she arrived in New York that she regarded the Liberty party as "dirty." Her remark raised such a protest in the antislavery societies that she had to take it back. She hadn't meant to say that the Liberty party was any dirtier than other political parties, she explained in a letter published in *The Liberator*. It was just dirtier than the American Anti-Slavery Society, for example.

Visiting among the New York abolitionists, Abby began to wonder if, in fact, the Liberty party was such an awful thing as the Garrisonians seemed to believe. "There will still be elections to the final Jubilee," she wrote her constant correspondent and mentor, Maria Chapman. "Should not abolitionists support candidates of whatever party who are not members of a proslavery church?" She proposed a teetotal pledge for abolitionists; they would support only antislavery candidates.

It is only the leaders of the Liberty party who are unsound, she told Maria. The people here are as good abolitionists as members of the Old Organization.

Gerrit Smith, an old friend of Abby's from the American Anti-Slavery meetings, was a major supporter of the Liberty party. In the summer of 1843 he offered to pay Abby's salary and expenses for three months, thus admitting the help she was to his movement. Abby turned him down haughtily. "I cannot identify myself with the Liberty Party," she wrote, ". . . because its policy in itself is an impediment to the progress of the cause, and second . . . the party does give currency to the foulest slanders against the American Society . . ."

Nevertheless, it sounded to Maria, and the other members of the Boston clique, as though Abby was being used by "third partyism." They worried constantly about her orthodoxy.

Further complicating the campaign in New York State were problems of personnel. When Abby first arrived, she felt there was need for a strong hand at the helm and began to write to John Collins, general agent of the American Anti-Slavery Society, asking him to come and take charge.

Someone was needed to coordinate the work of many agents, orchestrate the holding of the antislavery conventions, and handle finances, she thought.

Collins, however, when he at last came, proved a disappointment. Like many reformers of the day, he was interested in many reforms simultaneously. Antislavery, temperance, women's rights, anarchism, pacifism, natural foods, and the development of small "utopias" or communes, all went together in the movement for a better society. Every reformer, someone remarked, in those days had a special plan for a new community in his hip pocket.

In the case of Collins, the interest in the establishment of a new community became overriding. Shortly after he came to New York, he began to devote more and more time to a communitarian experiment in Skaneateles. Trying to continue with this interest, and still keep up the antislavery work, he was running all over the state, until Abby called him a "perpetual motion machine" and wrote to the officers of the Society that they should send someone to provide balance.

"Where is Collins the general agent that he does not keep the wheels in motion?" she asked of Maria Chapman. "O! The association question is of vastly greater importance . . . and therefore he is at Utica at the association meeting." The society had no one to send to "balance Collins." It finally became necessary for Abby to take over the campaign. Her organizational talents began to receive recognition from this date. She was a rising star in the abolitionist world.

Abby herself was sympathetic with the idea of forming intentional communities, but wasn't sure she would be comfortable living in one. "I don't like all the mixing up," she wrote. Two of Abby's older sisters, Diana and Joanna, who had married into the Ballou family, participated for several years in a communal living experiment at Hopedale, near Milford, Massachusetts, organized by another member of the family, Adin Ballou. Her friend Paulina Wright, with her husband, Francis Wright, moved into a community and then moved out again, disillusioned. One of the members had turned out to be a bigot. Abby had no time for such experiments. In her life there was really only one cause, antislavery.

For the sake of the cause she became a prodigious money-raiser. In July of 1843 James Gibbons, publisher of the *National Anti-Slavery Standard,* wrote to her gloomily about the coming bankruptcy of the American Anti-Slavery Society. The Boston clique came to the New York meetings, promised to raise money, then went off again and did nothing, he complained. The *Standard* was in danger of folding. Last week his printer had begged for fifty cents with which to buy bread for his hungry children.

Spurred on by his plea, Abby pledged herself to raise $2,500 for the society to support the paper, though often her donations came in the form of nickels and dimes. She wrote to a friend asking for advice about selling her paternal acres in Millbury in a hurry in order to raise money. And she began to worry about the quality of the *Standard* itself, fearing that it was not well enough edited to command a growing audience.

Lydia Maria Child, at odds with the board of the American Anti-Slavery Society, had been replaced by her husband, David Child. David was a staunch Whig; Abby considered him altogether too much a political being to represent the antislavery cause. David for his part did not like "comeouters" and attacked them in a blistering editorial published in

August 1843 in the *Standard*. Garrison made it worse by reprinting the article in *The Liberator* without comment.

This was too much for Abby. Wasn't she working day and night for the Old Organization? Shouldn't she be listened to? She wrote impassioned letters to both Garrison and Maria Chapman. Not getting the answers she wanted, she decided she had better visit Boston.

Starting off from Buffalo, where she had picked up a bad cold from standing in the spray of Niagara Falls, she traveled by railroad car to Rochester, and from there to Waterloo. Wrapped in her great, soft green shawl, she managed to sweat out her fever, but she was too weak and sick for several days to continue her journey. She recuperated at the home of the McClintocks, an antislavery family, at Waterloo, then went by painful stages to Utica, to Albany, to Springfield, to North-ampton, and so to Boston.

"I hate traveling, I am sick of it," she wrote a friend. "But union of effort is necessary and must be had. This belief sends me on my hateful journey."

But if Abby were coming east to straighten out the matter of David Child, the Bostonians saw it as their chance to straighten out Abby. They could hardly let her get a night's rest after reaching Boston before starting on a campaign to restore her to orthodoxy. It ended in a draw. Abby admitted she might have been sometimes naïve about the Liberty party. But she refused to patch things up with David Child, as Maria wanted her to do, and instead kept up her campaign of criticism until he was let go the following spring.

Returning to New York State from this brief trip to Mecca, Abby was able to make good her pledge to fight the Liberty party within a few weeks. At a Central New York State

Convention, held in Winfield in October, she outmaneuvered Alvan Stewart, the leader of the New Organizationists, and persuaded the group to express its allegiance to the American Anti-Slavery Society. Stewart tried to fight back by offering a resolution that it was the duty of all abolitionists to vote, but Abby had enough followers to defeat the motion.

After just a little over a year in New York, she had become a powerful figure in abolitionist circles. Even the Garrisonians had learned that though loyal, she was independent. At thirty-two, Abby was a woman to be reckoned with.

Abby Kelley Foster
*Brown Brothers*

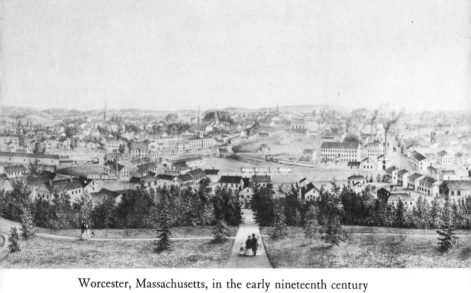

Worcester, Massachusetts, in the early nineteenth century
*The American Antiquarian Society*

William Lloyd Garrison

*Courtesy of The New-York Historical Society, New York City*

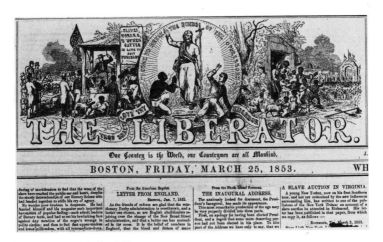

Masthead of *The Liberator*
Courtesy of *The New-York Historical Society, New York City*

New York City in 1836          *Museum of the City of New York*

Lucretia Mott
*Courtesy of The New-York Historical Society, New York City*

The burning of Pennsylvania Hall, May 17, 1838
*Courtesy of The Historical Society of Pennsylvania*

Twelve "eminent opponents of the slave power." *Clockwise*: John Quincy Adams, William Lloyd Garrison, Joshua R. Giddings, Cassius M. Clay, Benjamin Lundy, Owen Lovejoy, Gerrit Smith, William Cullen Bryant, Henry Ward Beecher. *Center*: John Greenleaf Whittier, Charles Sumner, Wendell Phillips

*Courtesy of The New-York Historical Society, New York City*

Stephen S. Foster as an old man
*Culver Pictures*

Lucy Stone
*Culver Pictures*

Oberlin College as it looked when Abby and Stephen spoke there in 1846
*The New York Public Library/Picture Collection*

Susan B. Anthony

*Courtesy of The New-York Historical Society, New York City*

Yᴱ MAY SESSION OF Yᴱ WOMAN'S RIGHTS CONVENTION—Yᴱ ORATOR OF Yᴱ DAY DENOUNCING Yᴱ LORDS OF CREATION.

A satirical contemporary view of the women's movement
*Courtesy of The New-York Historical Society, New York City*

John Brown captured by the U.S. Marines at Harpers Ferry
*Culver Pictures*

The black community of Washington, D.C., celebrating the abolition of slavery
*Courtesy of The New-York Historical Society, New York City*

# IX

## *A Matter of the Heart*

IN addition to fighting the Liberty party, Abby had another matter on her mind throughout most of the time she was in New York State. She had not forgotten her admiration for Stephen S. Foster, the radical "ultra." Now he was in New York State, also lecturing, and their trails began to cross frequently.

In November 1842, both Abby and Stephen attended an antislavery convention in Utica. Abby was in top form. *The American Express* wrote lyrically about her appearance: "She is a very intelligent looking person with a clear blue eye, a delicate complexion, fair hair, and a ladylike hand. Her voice is musical and her smile expressive." Stephen, on the other hand, was at the end of a long campaign, and on the point of exhaustion. His expressions had become more violent. Even his comrades he called "fools and liars" if they differed with him, and the church was "a den of Satan."

Privately, they were glad to see each other again, but publicly they tangled. Early in the convention Stephen offered a resolution that the abolitionists recognize the equal right of all present to participate in the discussions and deliberations of the group.

Abby rose to her feet and said she objected to the word deliberations. "We must have wide open discussion but when it comes to decision only members should vote," she declared. Let the word *deliberations* be struck and she would support the resolution.

Stephen rejoined that he did not believe in limiting the freedom of speech of anyone present.

The abolitionists present listened in fascination as two of the ablest antislavery lecturers began to debate the issue. Would Abby, with her logical mind and withering tongue, or Stephen, with his denunciations, win?

Before the discussion grew bitter, however, William Lloyd Garrison rose to support Abby. His influence was enough to swing the convention. The word *deliberations* was struck, and Foster's resolution passed without it.

Stephen apparently accepted his defeat with good grace, though later in the convention he made a short address "castigating those who would restrain free speech."

Foster was not only exhausted, he was ill. Shortly after the convention he went home to New Hampshire to recuperate. Abby began to write him long letters inquiring about his health, giving him advice. Why didn't he follow her example and try to eat nothing but breads and pastries made with Graham flour? Why did he insist on rising from his sickbed to go to more antislavery meetings? She had a good mind to write to his mother and ask her to keep him at home!

When Stephen wrote back that he had gone on a diet of completely raw foods, Abby thought he had gone too far. "I certainly will be cautious how I challenge you again . . . you are indeed a hard one," she chided him. Elsewhere she urged him to cheer up, throw himself wholeheartedly into recreation, and rest up for the long lifetime of reform which lay ahead. Slavery, she pointed out, was a "mere speck in the disk of moral law"; once slavery was ended there would remain "thick clouds and deep blackness to remove."

Abby was staying with Paulina and Francis Wright in Utica much of this time. The Wrights wrote to Stephen also. They reported to him on a phrenological study of his character done by a Dr. Fowler, which was later published in *The Liberator*. They told him that the three of them often "magnetized" each other at night, a process whereby electric impulses were supposed to run from one brain to another. Paulina was clearly Abby's confidante in her dealings with Stephen. The two women established a warm friendship, which lasted a lifetime, on this basis.

Throughout the winter and spring of 1843, Abby continued to write Stephen, apologizing that her letters to him were longer and more frequent than his to her. It was because she could not condense her thoughts, she explained. She used ten words to do the work of five. "Cannot you make me a thought-condensing machine?" she begged.

When Stephen wrote back, asking when they might meet again, Abby suggested that he come to the anniversary meeting in New York in May. They might be able to take a walk in that place "where, above all others, two can be alone." She told him that there was a rumor going around that she was going to marry some person in Massachusetts, and this rumor would protect them, as long as Stephen managed to keep "mum."

It was not until midsummer, however, that the two became engaged, after spending "a never-to-be-forgotten evening," in the front parlor of the Wrights' new house in Syracuse. Abby was happy but stern. She told Stephen that she was confessing her feelings to him only because she was sure he would not try to swerve her from the course of duty. She must crucify her desire for domestic life for the present, and continue to work for the poor slave. They must keep their relationship a secret. If it were in the open, and society permitted them spending a great deal of time together, Abby did not know whether or not she could contain her ardent feelings for long.

Stephen listened, but it was, as Abby described it, a mesmeric evening, and he was evidently mesmerized, for a few days later he wrote to her reproaching her for wanting to hide their love. "Are you not conscious of a feeling of reluctance at the thought of sharing with me the reproach and contempt which my course of life has incurred?" he inquired.

Nothing could have wounded Abby more. How could she, herself the object of so much scorn, fear to share public censure with Stephen? No, she would follow him to prison, or to the stake, if need be. "But my slave sister's tenderest affections are trampled and for her sake I smother mine for the present," she told him piously.

All through the summer they continued to exchange love letters. By August Stephen was finally convinced that Abby really was going to marry him—that the secrecy she imposed would not last forever. In a jubilant frame of mind, he wrote a long letter boasting that he had won her honestly and now intended to claim her as his own. He planned "to take possession of his new property by Christmas," he told Abby.

He was joking about the property, but serious about the timing.

"I have no idea of spending another cold winter alone, so long as I have a wife who is bound to dwell with me and keep me warm and comfortable. I am heartsick of bricks and flat irons for winter companions. They may do for you, but they will not do for me. I have had them long enough, and now I must have my Abby."

The letter was seven pages long, and equally ardent throughout. It was delivered to Abby while she was sitting on the stage of an antislavery meeting. Earlier she had announced that Stephen Foster might be coming into the area shortly to join the campaign. Now she tore open the letter and in front of the large audience read through the torrid prose, looking for news. She finally looked up in confusion and said she could not say whether or not Foster was coming, it would be announced later.

Stephen's talk of an earlier marriage date bewildered her. Had she not made it clear that they must wait? "I will be slow to sit down to the banquet of domestic sweets while I know the only music I can hear at that banquet will be the wail of the southern wife and the long groan of her heartbroken husband at the long distance that separates them," she wrote. "My dearest friend, will you tell me frankly whether you have not been jesting in this letter, and if you have not, will you retract what you have said about Christmas?" she begged. Lacking herself the slightest sense of humor, Abby never knew when others were joking with her.

Stephen did indeed retract his demand, and thereafter he did what he could to accommodate himself to Abby's decision that they could not be married for at least two years, possibly until Jubilee. He could never quite follow her reasoning, but to Abby it was clear that marriage was a trap. It might swallow her up, as it had Angelina Grimké. She must not waver from the path of duty. Her own deeply felt identification with the lot of the slave forbade it. How could the man she loved because of his high principles ask it of her?

No, they must either see little of each other or, if they were together, treat each other as brother and sister. Indeed, she was determined to rule her feelings so that they might continue to work together. By following the rules of the Moral Reform Society of which they were both members, avoiding staying up together late at night, and working wholeheartedly in the cause, they would bury their feelings from the sight of all.

Their love for each other fed their oratory, and both were in top form that first summer. "The place is now launched to a perfect fury," Abby wrote to Maria Chapman. "I get up a storm and S. S. Foster comes along and increases it to a tempest."

Now that she and Stephen were secretly engaged, Abby's dearest wish was that he be reconciled with the Boston Garrisonians. Maria Chapman's opinion she particularly valued. Earlier, Abby had written to Stephen optimistically that she believed the prejudices against him were wearing away. She urged him to get to know Mrs. Chapman better, and wrote to Maria to sing his praises.

The Bostonians, however, would have none of it. Radical they might be, but they clung to their reputation for gentility and respectability. It was this Stephen threatened with his wild language and behavior. Maria wrote Abby a long letter criticizing Stephen, saying that he could always be counted on "to blunder forward to the destruction of the American Society."

Torn between her lover and her friend, Abby showed the letter to Stephen. It did not help matters in the slightest, and she later regretted her hasty action. Characteristically, however, she did not give way before Stephen's anger. Maria was a good and wise woman, she told him; the only problem was that she did not know Stephen very well, and therefore thought him a fool.

While Stephen recuperated from exhaustion, he wrote a pamphlet consolidating his attacks on the church. *The Brotherhood of Thieves, or a True Picture of the American Church and Clergy*, published in 1843, was a shocker—and a bestseller. In it Stephen accused the churches of condoning, and therefore in fact practicing, theft, adultery, manstealing, piracy, and murder. The Quakers were as bad as the rest; while professing to abhor slavery they went to the polls and voted for proslavery candidates.

Abby welcomed the pamphlet and sold it at her antislavery meetings. The other abolitionists, however, were more critical. *The Brotherhood of Thieves*, coupled with Stephen's continuing interruption of church services, carried anticlericalism to ridiculous extremes, they thought.

Stephen's penchant for martyrdom, abrasive language, illogical stands, and plain bad taste upset many. Lydia Maria Child once wrote that "Stephen Foster will be as good as an unleashed bulldog to keep me away from the Anti-Slavery meetings," and Maria Chapman quipped, "God makes use of instruments I wouldn't touch with a pair of tongs."

The Bostonians also worried that Stephen was influencing

Abby toward the Liberty party. When she went with him to a
Liberty party convention in Buffalo, they were sure of it.
Stephen himself was an ardent critic of voting at all. He
believed that to acknowledge the state, while it upheld
slaveholding, was to be guilty of condoning slavery. Still, he
reasoned, if men must vote, then the Liberty party at least
gave them an opportunity to avoid voting for proslavery
candidates.

Stephen was, in fact, attracted to political action, despite his
principled objections to it. Several times he dabbled with the
antislavery political parties, hoping each time he could use
them, and not they him.

At first, Maria Chapman tried to use her influence on Abby
to break up the budding romance. She began to argue that
Abby was wasting her time in New York State and ought to
return to the New England area. This Abby refused to do.
After her trip to Boston in September 1843, she tried to
prevent the Liberty party from gathering up converts in her
trail, but she and Stephen continued to stump New York
State, sometimes together, sometimes apart, until the early
months of 1844. Together they were a great team. Whether or
not people suspected the real nature of their relationship, the
names of Abby Kelley and Stephen Foster were more and
more linked as a fiery twosome, guaranteed to turn a town
upside down.

Under Stephen's influence, Abby's anticlericalism grew. A
woman in Seneca Falls, one of her converts, had been
excommunicated for going to her meetings, and this fed the
fire. At the First Annual Meeting of the Western Anti-Slavery
Society, held in Rochester in late 1843, Abby offered a
resolution to the effect that the church organization and clergy

of the North "are responsible for the sighs, shrieks, groans, heathen darkness, pollutions, and blood of the South."

It was a far cry from her earlier, simple, biblical speeches. She was becoming a true "fanatick."

# X

# *The Campaign Continues*

THE year 1844 saw a presidential election. At issue were a dispute with Great Britain over the boundaries of the Oregon territory, and the annexation of Texas. The abolitionists had been bitterly opposed to this annexation for many years. Texas, they believed, might be carved into several states, all proslavery, thus upsetting the delicate balance between slave and free states established by the Missouri Compromise. At the same time it would probably lead to war with Mexico—a war the nonresistance movement opposed.

The Whigs nominated Henry Clay; the Democrats, James Polk; the Liberty party, James Birney. In 1840 the Liberty party had been new, and something of a joke. In 1844 it was strong enough to carry New York and take enough votes away from Clay to give the election to Polk.

As the campaign began to heat up in the early spring of 1844, it became finally clear to Abby that she was not going to persuade the New York abolitionists to stay away from the polls. If she were no longer to be a tool of the Liberty party, she ought to get out of the state. Stephen came to the same conclusion, and the two returned east: Stephen to Rhode Island, Abby to Massachusetts.

Happy in her love affair, happy to be home, Abby was in top form. She continued to make converts. In the town of New Brookfield, Massachusetts, she met a young woman, Lucy Stone, who was planning to attend Oberlin College the next year. Impressed by Lucy, Abby invited her to come and sit beside her in the pulpit at an antislavery lecture. "O, I can't," Lucy replied. "I have ridden three miles, and my hair is all blown about." "O Lucy," Abby said, "you are not half emancipated."

Deeply impressed by Abby, Lucy later became an antislavery lecturer, then one of the inspired great leaders of the women's rights movement. Although they had their differences, the two women were lifelong friends.

Lecturing several times each day, going from town to town, Abby was frequently exhausted. Stephen managed to meet Abby in Massachusetts in March and was distressed by what he saw. She was working far too hard, eating too little, losing weight. She was, in short, a fit candidate for tuberculosis. Last year she had seen the danger for him and had urged him to go home and rest, he reminded her. He had obeyed, and was now restored to health. But she herself would pay no attention to his warnings.

"I have no doubt that my present labors are bringing me to a premature grave," he wrote lugubriously, "and yet they are light compared to yours. And besides you are guilty of constant exposures of your person against which the strongest system cannot long endure.

"It is mainly for regard to your health and my own, but

especially yours that I have urged a declaration of our marriage. Not that I do not long, ardently long, to clasp you in my arms and press you to my bosom to be torn from it no more, but I could endure our separation for the present, painful as it is, but for the consciousness that you are hastening to an untimely fate."

Abby answered Stephen immediately, to assure him of her good health and to say that his letter made her laugh. It was *she* who was worried about *him*. Let them both take care of themselves, and let Stephen stop worrying. He should instead "laugh and grow fat."

Concern for each other's health continued to be a constant theme in their letters. They both drove themselves beyond average human endurance, and were subject to colds, sore throats, fevers, and upset stomachs. Both were also mild hypochondriacs, willing to try the newest fads in health foods and water treatments and to listen to any new theory about human bodily functions.

Recovered in health at least temporarily, the two lovers were united briefly when they both attended the anniversary meeting of the American Anti-Slavery Society, held as usual in New York City.

Abby's fame as a speaker was now such that people came to these sessions especially to hear her. This year she lashed out bitterly at the New Organization, calling Charles W. Denison, one of its organizers, a true Benedict Arnold. The New Organization had run off with the society's money and its official newspaper, she claimed. The slaves would be freed now if the split hadn't occurred!

"And Denison claims that is due to his respect for woman and he would put a padlock on her lips in public," she scoffed.

"They [the New Organizationists] would take away her right of speech, which she values more than personal liberty, and which she has resolved to maintain to the last."

From New York, Stephen returned to his native New Hampshire, and Abby to Massachusetts. By July, however, she changed her mind and made her headquarters in Durham, New Hampshire. It caused talk. Joanna Ballou, Abby's older sister, scolded her for not staying away from Stephen and said she thought if Abby would conduct herself properly in the future "your character may be in some measure retrieved." Another sister wrote suggesting that she "be prudent and not get into any bad scrapes."

Abby's only defense against slander was to keep a companion with her at all times. She was delighted when Jane Elizabeth Hitchcock of Oneida, New York, came to join her in New Hampshire. She had asked for Lizzie's company before, but Lizzie's brothers had been opposed. They were interested in forming an experimental community in New York State and wanted Lizzie with them. Now, however, Lizzie insisted. Abby found later that she could be a bit stubborn. Nevertheless, the two got along well, and Lizzie learned a great deal from Abby, becoming a famous woman orator in later years.

In New Hampshire the local papers found Abby good copy. The Portsmouth *Journal* called her a modern Amazon and thought her intelligent and a skilled orator, though they had to disagree with her attacks on church and state. The Exeter *News Letter*, however, suggested she was an exhibitionist: "She wrung her hands . . . stamped her feet . . . smote the desk . . . shook her garments . . . struck her breast . . . courted notice . . . and defied opposition."

In truth, Abby had by this time developed a whole repertoire of styles. She often changed her approach as the occasion seemed to warrant, though she still tried to be led by the Inner Light. She could be cool, reasonable, and sweet, as she had been at the beginning of her lectures. Or she could be as dramatic as an actress, as harsh and condemning as Stephen himself. She was in fact a seasoned orator, and she spoke not to please newspaper reporters, but to sway crowds.

Everywhere, Garrison abolitionists needed her as their spokeswoman. Throughout the fall of 1844 she received letters urging her to come to Pennsylvania, where the Liberty party was getting a foothold under the leadership of Thomas Earle. Abby, however, put off the trip until after Election Day. Stephen, who was involved in a struggle within the New Hampshire Anti-Slavery Society over the ownership of the newspaper the *Herald of Freedom*, needed her support and though they were rarely together, she liked working in the same state as he.

No sooner had she agreed that she would visit Pennsylvania, however, than she began to receive advice about how she must conduct herself and her campaign there. The advice was well-meant, but Abby was irritated. "The Philadelphians all think the truth is as tender as eggs and should be handled much more carefully, for fear it might be annihilated and they think no one can handle it properly but under their direction," she complained to Stephen. "I have all along, expecting many and important curtain lectures after arriving on the enchanted ground, but as I have made up my mind to receive it all in good part into my ear, and then go and do as my judgment and conscience shall dictate, I am under no anxiety."

Finally, after the December 4 election was over, and a short visit with her relatives in Connecticut, she and Lizzie Hitchcock took the steamer from Norwich to Long Island, the Long Island Rail Road to New York City, and a boat the next day to Philadelphia. They traveled in the forward deck, which was reserved for blacks and called the Jim Crow deck. Like some other abolitionists, Abby always traveled Jim Crow as a gesture when she could, and sometimes met new friends in this manner.

They arrived in Philadelphia at one o'clock on a winter afternoon, and after a brief rest Abby was ready for her first debate with the lawyer and Liberty party organizer, Thomas Earle, that night. Though the election was over and Polk had won, the debate between voting and nonvoting abolitionists continued. Abby argued with him in Philadelphia and in Bucks and Montgomery counties in the following days.

"Earle's main object was to make up false issues and divert attention from the main point constantly," Abby wrote Stephen. "In fine it was confusion worse confounded. All I could do was constantly to keep before people the idea that Liberty Party is not an anti-slavery instrumentality and that it was our first and worst foe. . . . I told them that if suitable opportunity should present I should show that Liberty Party is to the Anti-Slavery Cause now, what Colonization was a few years ago."

Abby thought Thomas Earle was "unprincipled" and "unfair in debate." Several of the local abolitionists, in fact, refused to appear with him. Nevertheless, she did not hesitate to take him on. Several times she felt she was able to sway the audience to her side, despite his polished arguments. Women were delighted to see that a woman was capable of defeating the famous Earle.

For the next three months Abby spoke almost every night in one town or another of eastern Pennsylvania, traveling from Bucks to Montgomery to Delaware to Chester counties, and visiting Lancaster, an abolitionist stronghold. In February she lectured in Wilmington, Delaware, under the sponsorship of the famous conductor of the underground railroad Thomas Garrett. The Wilmington abolitionists were upset by her fellow lecturer, Dr. Hudson, but felt Abby's "better language, softer voice, and feebler manner" had greater appeal. In March she charmed audiences in West Chester, Pennsylvania. "She is fluent in speech, her gesticulations are graceful, and appropriate, and at times she grows truly eloquent," the local paper, *The Jeffersonian*, reported.

As usual, Abby was also fundraising. "Bleed those fat Quakers," Wendell Phillips wrote her. "Do your utmost. I never need urge you." Abby found the Quakers "generous with everything but money." Nevertheless she enjoyed herself thoroughly. "The Pennsylvania Quakers are the kindest people on earth," she reported.

In January she wrote Stephen urging him to come immediately. New York, where he was considering going next, was a hopeless field for him, while Pennsylvania was in the best possible condition for his labors. The milder climate suited her, and she was sure it would be better for him. He might even find land here on which eventually to farm. We don't need to be together, she argued, and so "no talk will come of our improprieties."

Stephen wrote back huffily that he was still needed in New Hampshire. Anyway, since Abby had refused to marry him, he was an old bachelor once more. This wounded her. "You may have assumed your old bachelor habits and feelings but I frankly confess I cannot again be an old maid," she wrote. "I want to see my other half more than ever before. Come now, Stephen, don't be so offish but carry yourself like a gallant knight toward your lady and toward the cause. Don't pout so, merely because I can't afford to marry till next winter."

Abby had decided that if she were to be married she must have an adequate trousseau of household linens. Since she had given away her whole inheritance to the antislavery cause, she had to scrape up spare cash to buy the materials. Whenever she had an extra moment during the next year, she spent it hemming.

Stephen overcame his offishness and arrived in the Philadelphia area early in March. The lovers had a rendezvous in New Jersey, then took separate campaign trails. "Do you not feel happier for our last interview?" Abby wrote. "I cannot think long absence will make you more comfortable. What a strange man you are if it is so. Let me see my beloved as often as possible. Every day's absence but strengthens the longings of my heart for its cherished object. How happy I will be that day which shall say that separation shall no longer be necessary."

Throughout the early spring Abby continued to travel from settlement to settlement in the beautiful rolling hills of Chester and Lancaster counties, with Lizzie, Dr. Hudson, and Benjamin Jones, a young Quaker abolitionist.

Benjie and Lizzie often spoke together, and sometimes came home spattered with rotten eggs. Soon a romance developed. Abby watched it with indulgent eyes. In love herself, she was glad to see others in the same happy state. As often as she could tactfully do so, she encouraged the two to take Dr. Hudson along on speaking engagements, while she stayed at home to write letters. Her popularity was such that if she were present no one else was permitted to speak. Dr. Hudson was particularly unpopular in the area and was often hurt when the crowd insisted on his keeping quiet and letting Abby be heard.

Remaining at home thus one day at the house of a wealthy Chester County abolitionist, Abby had a chat with the family's Irish maid. The poor girl earned only one dollar a week and was asked to do all the work of the house, the mistress not stirring herself so much as to make her own bed. In addition, the servant was treated like a slave and shut up in a desolate kitchen as an outcast.

It was not an atypical story. The Irish, having arrived in the United States in large numbers at this time, were the most oppressed and exploited people in the Northern states.

"When I talked with her and tried to console her and told her that we were trying to bring about a better state of things, a state in which she would be regarded as an equal, she wept like a child and sounded full of gratitude," Abby wrote Stephen. "I think, Stephen, we should be faithful in the families where we go and bear testimony against this great wickedness. I have been negligent."

It was the beginning for Abby of a widening of her circle of concern. The slave first, oppressed women next, the "servile" white worker third—these were her priorities.

Still another romance claimed Abby's divided attention that spring. Her young friend Lizzie Neall, recently ill with tuberculosis, was secretly engaged to Sydney Howard Gay. Gay was a good friend of Abby's, and she was delighted that he had been selected as the new editor of the *National Anti-Slavery Standard.* Unfortunately, Lizzie's father, Daniel

Neall, disapproved of the match. Abby wrote to Lizzie counseling patience. Your father will come to love Sydney, she predicted. "I know what it is to crucify my feelings and can sympathize fully with thee."

By this time Abby's engagement to Stephen was no longer a secret. Several groups of friends urged Abby to delay the wedding no longer and offered to have the ceremony at their homes. A young woman admirer from Fallowfield, Pennsylvania, wrote to say how glad she was to know that Stephen was looking for land in that vicinity, and how warmly she would welcome Abby as a neighbor. Stephen himself confided to his brother, Galen, that they would be married in late fall or early winter.

"Abby sends you an invitation to her wedding, which she says will come about Christmas at Kennett, Chester County, Pennsylvania," he wrote. "I shall not join her in this at present at least; for I think it a matter of great doubt whether she ever has one. I am a great friend of marriage but have little sympathy with weddings."

Stephen believed that a marriage between a man and woman should be sanctioned by God alone, and that neither the church nor the state had anything to say in the matter. It was in keeping with his anarchistic, or "comeouter," beliefs. Any sort of wedding at all suggested that the private agreement between the couple required a public sanction.

Abby, however, continued to worry about her reputation and to fear that she and Stephen were suspected of believing in "no-marriage perfectionism." She therefore looked forward to some sort of a public ceremony which would prove to the world that this was not so.

Stephen was a determined man, but he knew that he would

have trouble holding out against Abby's persuasive powers. By falling in love with this extraordinary woman, he had sacrificed his freedom to please only himself and his conscience.

"It is impossible to foresee what influence she will exert over me previous to that time," he wrote Galen. "She may possibly so far reconcile me to them [weddings] as to induce me to become a party to one."

# XI

# *The* Anti-Slavery Bugle

ONCE more Abby Kelley was called to new fields. In March an invitation came to attend the Ohio Anti-Slavery Anniversary meeting, to be held in New Lisbon in June, and to stay on for a series of conventions in various parts of the state. The more Abby thought about it, the more she felt it would be a good place for her to spend the summer. She would be apart from Stephen; she would work too hard to miss him and still have time in which to finish hemming the linens of her trousseau.

After the anniversary meeting in New York, she and Stephen spent a week together at the home of friends in Plymouth, Massachusetts. Rested, she was then ready for the trip. Lizzie Hitchcock and Benjamin Jones were to join her in Ohio, as well as a newcomer, Giles Stebbins, a young antislavery lecturer based in western New York. The trip, however, she was to make alone.

She traveled in stages, stopping at Albany, Utica, Syracuse, and Rochester, and going most of the way by canal boat. She liked the way the boat "slipped along through the countryside so quietly and smoothly." But she was often the only passenger and did not enjoy sitting down alone and "eating my Graham food in dumb silence." She had concluded that it was not good for women to eat alone, though she enjoyed being alone in her chamber at night.

Arriving in Ohio, she was favorably impressed with the Buckeyes. She liked their candor, she wrote. "The most marked distinction between New England and Ohio is that here all deformities and incongruities are visible to the whole world, there they are covered and glossed over. I like the openness."

On this and subsequent visits to Ohio, Abby spent most of her time in the northeastern section, known at the time as the Western Reserve, and settled by New Englanders in the early years of the nineteenth century. The families from Connecticut and Massachusetts had brought with them New England architecture and New England customs, but the freedom of the frontier had affected manners in a few decades.

Abby's first stop in the Western Reserve was at Jefferson, the home of Joshua Giddings, an abolitionist, a Whig, and a member of Congress. The large-hearted Giddings was interested in all members of the antislavery movement and did not hold it against Garrison or Abby that they disapproved on principle with his serving elected office. Abby for her part liked Giddings as a person, and struck up a friendship with his daughter, Maria. Despite her usual high principles she did not scruple to use Giddings's friendship for her own ends, letting him help in setting up meetings where she later attacked all politicians, including Whigs.

"I admire him," she wrote a friend, ". . . as much as I can

admire a politician. He is as honest as a politician can be and more honest than I had expected to find him."

Because Abby was the guest of Giddings, she and Giles Stebbins were conveyed by the high sheriff of Ashtabula County (in the sheriff's hands already, Abby quipped) to Warren, where a local dignitary, Judge King, lost no time in calling on them.

Abby did not want to receive hospitality under false pretenses, so she immediately blurted out that she had come to Ohio to fight the Liberty party. The judge, who was evidently a Liberty man, did not blink an eyelash but insisted that Abby and Giles spend the night at his house. However, the next morning he announced that he was not going to be able to go with them to the anniversary meeting of the Ohio Anti-Slavery Society, held in New Lisbon, after all. Business detained him.

"I could not but query whether his business would have been so urgent," Abby wrote Stephen, "if we had not come."

New Lisbon was the county seat of Columbiana County. In 1845, when Abby first visited it, it had a population of 1,800, many of them Quakers.

The Ohio Anti-Slavery Society was new. It responded with fervor to Abby's evangelical appeal. In the midst of the general enthusiasm, the executive committee voted to found a paper, call it the *Anti-Slavery Bugle,* and pay its editor four hundred dollars a year.

Abby was delighted. She believed strongly that a good paper, with sound principles, was necessary to hold together the antislavery converts which she made. She immediately wrote to friends in the East, urging them to lend support. Would not Parker Pillsbury come out and give Milo

Townsend, the new editor, a hand in getting started? She admired Townsend's appearance but feared he would lack energy alone.

Although she had just parted from Stephen, with the resolution to stay away from him until it was time to be married, it suddenly seemed to her that he, too, was badly needed in Ohio. "They want you here and have often asked if you could not be induced to come," she wrote him disingenuously.

Stephen had planned his summer apart from Abby with care. He was committed to working for the antislavery society in New Hampshire in July. Thereafter he would try to earn some money for their approaching marriage, by either farming or teaching school, or by any other lucrative employment he could find. Abby's appeal, however, was too strong for his resolves. By mid-July he had joined her, and thereafter they were together, let tongues wag as they might.

Parker Pillsbury, however, did not come, and Milo Townsend decided he could not live on four hundred dollars a year as editor of the *Bugle*. Abby wrote to Maria in July, begging her help in getting an editor for the new paper. Would Wendell Phillips come? How about Oliver Johnson? Wouldn't the American Society pay the editor's salary? It was imperative that the paper get off to a good start.

Meanwhile she put her young friends Benjamin Jones and Lizzie Hitchcock at work getting out the first edition. Benjamin threw himself into the enterprise with such enthusiasm that Lizzie wrote that she was jealous of the paper. Abby thought they did pretty well for amateurs, but continued to pester her Eastern colleagues for a seasoned editor. For one thing, she observed, it would be better to have Benjamin and Lizzie lecturing.

The lecturing was going well. Early in July, Joshua Giddings set up a series of meetings in his district. Abby and Giles Stebbins startled their audiences by attacking both church and state vigorously, but the novelty of a woman speaker, and the appeal of their unusual views, brought them large crowds.

On the Fourth of July, Giddings arranged for them to speak in a church at Jefferson. He had, he confessed to Abby, a perfect loathing for the old powder-burning, bell-ringing celebrations of Independence Day, but had never dared discourage them until Abby's coming gave him the opportunity. On this Fourth, the only bell rung in the village was the bell calling people to church to hear the abolitionists.

On subsequent days, they spoke in courtyards, in town squares, in open groves. Abby had to raise her voice to be heard in such surroundings, but her lungs were now as strong as a sailor's. There was a great stirring-up, as she wrote her friends. Their attacks on the Liberty party were gratifying to the ears of the Whigs in her audiences, still smarting from having lost the last election because of the inroads of the Liberty party vote.

The country was in a great state of excitement in July of 1845. The people of the Republic of Texas had just voted for annexation to the United States, and an Eastern magazine, the *United States Magazine and Democratic View,* had published an unsigned editorial declaring that it was "the Manifest Destiny of the United States to overspread the entire continent." It looked very much as though the long fight against annexation was lost, and war with Mexico was near.

Abby did not concentrate on these issues. She was still more concerned with the fundamental questions: the role of church and state in upholding slavery. Nevertheless she alluded to the current situation and further aroused the emotions of her antislavery audiences.

"We are having rich times, here, I can assure you," Abby wrote to Sydney Howard Gay, now editor of the *Standard.* "The Whigs hear, through Giddings, that we are doing great service and so they come from far and near to induce us to visit their respective places. We go in under the patronage of their tall men and then the way we deal out our blows right and left is a caution to Whigs and Democrats as well as Liberty Party. All hands are thrown into straits and the way Stephen clinches the nails which the rest of us drive would do your soul good to witness."

Though Abby praised Stephen, it was beginning to be noticed in Ohio that she was the principal personage of the two. Her striking looks and dramatic style commanded the most attention. Stephen had been in his heyday when he broke up church meetings and shocked the pious with his wild accusations. He was less comfortable in the role of lecturer day after day, and spoke more frequently of becoming a farmer instead.

If Stephen was becoming quieter, Abby was beginning to adopt his radical techniques. In August she attended the Yearly Meeting of the Society of Friends of Ohio held at Mount Pleasant, a Quaker settlement near the West Virginia border. The large, barnlike meetinghouse had been recently built, but the meeting itself was torn with dissension between two conflicting movements within Quakerism at the time. In the silence, the atmosphere crackled with tension.

Abby sat through the first morning quietly, but toward the end of the afternoon rose and began to remind the Quakers of their historical witness against slavery. She had only spoken a few moments when the presiding clerk asked her to sit down and not disturb the meeting.

"I have been given a message to deliver, whether you will hear me or not," Abby responded. She began again, only to be interrupted by another elder.

"A sense of propriety and good order requires that thee take a seat," he told her sternly.

"I would remind Friends that George Fox also felt under the weight of the Lord to interrupt church services," Abby responded tartly.

"If thee doesn't sit down we will have to carry thee out," another Friend shouted.

"If you must go to such lengths to deny the truth, go ahead," Abby replied.

Several men approached Abby and attempted to lead her from the room. She had learned her lesson well, however, and instead of cooperating, went limp. In a scene of great confusion, which many Friends found unbearably disgraceful, she was picked up and carried bodily from the meetinghouse, several women plucking at her clothes, and laid on the cool grass outside.

After a few moments she picked herself up, shaken but triumphant. She had witnessed to the truth against those very Quaker elders who had inspired her awe as a child. And she had been a true nonresistant when hands were laid upon her.

By fall Abby and Stephen had hoped to finish in Ohio and go back to their beloved New York State, where they were much needed. It soon became apparent to them, however, that they ought not to leave Ohio. The struggle to get subscribers and support for the *Anti-Slavery Bugle* was slow and strenuous. No help came from the East. Instead, Maria Chapman urged Abby, Stephen, and the rest to return to Massachusetts. Oliver Johnson was not interested in the job. In general the Eastern abolitionists seemed to be preoccupied with their own affairs and not much concerned in events so far away. It was clear that if the *Bugle* were to survive at all, Abby and Stephen were needed.

"We now have some seven hundred subscribers. We intend to have one thousand before we leave the state," Abby wrote her sister in the fall. For the sake of her beloved *Bugle* she was willing to go from house to house, collecting sums as small as quarters for subscriptions and donations.

Along with her plans to return to New York State, Abby had to sacrifice her dreams of a marriage in the East which friends and relatives could attend. "Tis a great disappointment, for since last spring I have looked forward to that occasion with great interest," Abby wrote her friend Lizzie Neall. "I wanted my friends present and I had a half proposition in my head to have an antislavery meeting called at Old Kennett and at its close have the ceremony performed in *church*—that all the world might know 'for certain' that S. S. Foster and Abby Kelley were not opposed to the marriage institution. But here we are and we must do the best we can. We shall probably be married in western Pennsylvania, in the house of one of our friends, sometime in December. We would invite our eastern friends, if we thought it would be of any use, or perhaps if we did not think they could use their money and time to better purpose in the cause, even if they felt disposed to come."

Actually, Abby was still having a hard time persuading Stephen to have any sort of marriage ceremony at all. Even the presence of relatives and close friends, he thought, smacked too much of an official societal sanction.

As a result Abby did not even invite her own sisters to her marriage, though she wrote Olive a long letter in November. She had looked up several of her older sisters and half-sisters in Ohio, and reported on their welfare. She had hoped to have some relatives at the wedding but "we make this sacrifice, for the slave's sake, as we have others, with joy."

Thus heralded, the marriage of Abby and Stephen Foster was finally accomplished on December 21, 1845, at the home of Milo Townsend at New Brighton, Pennsylvania, just over the Ohio border. Abby drew up a Quakerlike certificate, and the two married themselves without benefit of clergy or Quaker committee of oversight. The signatures of twelve witnesses were enough to make it a legal document. In deference to Stephen's antipathy for ceremonies, their public declaration was stark:

"Stephen S. Foster . . . and Abby Kelley . . . have this day—consummated a matrimonial connection in accordance with the divine law of marriage, by a public declaration of our mutual affection, and covenant of perpetual love and fidelity of our purpose to perform faithfully all the relative duties of husband and wife," the certificate read.

Of their close friends, only Benjamin Jones and Lizzie Hitchcock were present. (They themselves were married a few weeks later.) The occasion was very simple; no cake or wine was served.

Many years later Stephen revealed that on the day after the wedding the two had made a secret agreement that each was free to withdraw from the marriage at any time. Even he, however, apparently hesitated to make such a shocking proposition public in 1846.

After postponing it so long, Abby immediately decided that marriage was a better state than spinsterhood, even from the point of view of her beloved cause. To Lizzie Neall and Sydney Gay, who had been married the month before, she wrote happily, "I wish you to congratulate the cause on the fact that since our marriage our meetings have been much more successful than heretofore. We realize that even in the anti-slavery cause a whole man and a whole woman are far better than a half man and a half woman. Aside, were it not that you too are in the honeymoon I should barely have written the above for fear of a turned up nose. But God grant your honeymoon to last as long as ours will, i.e. through eternity."

Despite the rumors to the contrary, Abby and Stephen clearly waited until after their marriage to enter into an intimate relationship. After all the years of waiting, their union was ecstatic. Years later Stephen visited the farmhouse "where I first entered into the married state" and wrote rhapsodically of his memories of that occasion.

Abby and Stephen were scarcely happier than their friends. There had been so much talk, and so many false reports that a marriage had already taken place, that most of the abolitionists rejoiced to have them formally united at last. For their close friends it was a time of special joy, Abigail Mott from Albany telling of her happiness that they "have consummated your union, at least the form, which frees you from embarrassments. Your souls have long been united." Parker Pillsbury wrote to his best friend to congratulate him on the marriage. "Abby is after all *the woman* of the age," he said. To Abby he addressed his hope that she would continue to live for the antislavery enterprise as she had before. "I doubt if there was much joy in heaven when Theodore Weld ran away with both the Grimkés and made one a mother and the both obscure and private women as ever swung the distaff," he observed wryly.

He need not have worried. Marriage was not going to stop Abby Kelley. As Abby Kelley Foster, her fame was instead to grow.

# XII

# *Driven to Extremes*

WHEN Stephen, urging Abby to marry him, had accused her of reluctance to share his fate, she had been indignant. Wasn't she already the focus of reproach and contempt? she asked. Nevertheless, in her first year as Stephen's wife, Abby Kelley Foster was attacked more violently than she had been before. It destroyed what little moderation she had left, and drove her steadily into a more radical position.

The trouble began in late winter when Abby and Stephen, having had a long honeymoon and rest, began lecturing in the Western Reserve again. Late in February they arrived at Oberlin College, where they tried to arrange meetings for the faculty and students.

Founded in 1833, Oberlin was the first college in the United States to admit blacks and women. It had a strong antislavery bent and seemed a likely institution to welcome the Fosters.

Oberlin, however, was also strongly religious in the

conventional sense, or "clerical" as the Fosters would call it. When Abby and Stephen arrived, the college was in the midst of a religious revival. (Abby called it a revival of their superstitions.) Charles Finney, the college pastor, did not want competition from mere reformers while there were souls to save.

Denied a platform at Oberlin, Abby and Stephen moved their operations to the nearby small town of Elyria. Here, they met with students as well as many free blacks from the community. As usual, the Fosters not only preached against slavery but aired their views against voting, against the established church, against the observance of the Sabbath. To back up the latter position they passed out some pamphlets recently prepared on the subject.

Present at the Elyria meetings was Lucy Stone, the young woman Abby had met in West Brookfield two years earlier, now a student at Oberlin. For Lucy the meetings were a turning point in her life. "I wish I could tell you how much good I received from your visit here," she wrote. "My heart dances gaily at the remembrance. It will be long before I shall be so cheered up again."

Abby, on her part, was enchanted by Lucy. She called her a little wild flower and said she thought it was a miracle that she bloomed in the mire and under the murky sky of a heathenish religion. Could not Lucy be induced to become an antislavery lecturer, she inquired? After all, "one woman is worth two men any day in a moral movement." Later in the same letter she returned to the subject. "Would that the women could feel their responsibilities as they ought! . . . then we should see such progress of the principles as we have never yet witnessed. From some remark of yours I inferred that you contemplate trampling on prejudice and taking the field after the close of your course. Why delay?"

But if Abby was pleased with Lucy, she was less so with the news from Oberlin following her departure. Though Lucy wrote glowingly that the women were interested in the women's issue as a result of Abby's visit, she had to confess that the faculty continued to abuse the Fosters. In fact, the *Oberlin Evangelist* published an attack describing them as infidels. Elsewhere they were described as low, degraded, licentious vagabonds. Abby was stung as usual by such criticisms. She and Stephen would return to Oberlin and have it out with the faculty, she resolved.

Meanwhile, news from the Texas border indicated that the long-awaited, long-dreaded war with Mexico was near. On April 24 and again on May 3 there were skirmishes, and on May 11 President Polk delivered a war message claiming that "Mexico has shed American blood on American soil."

The House and Senate were debating the ratification of the war message just as the abolitionists were preparing to make their annual trek to New York to attend the anniversary meetings of the American Anti-Slavery Society. By the time the meetings were held, war had been declared, against the opposition of the Whigs.

Though heavy-hearted, the abolitionists proceeded with their meetings as planned. The first session was nearly ended when Abby rose to protest: "While the newsboys are crying at the corner of every street the tale of war . . . I don't think that this meeting should adjourn its first session without allusion to the subject. I did not come prepared to speak upon it, hence I have no resolution but . . . when we remember that this war is carried on for the purpose of perpetuating this bloody traffic in American daughters . . . an American woman may stand on the platform of the American Anti-Slavery Society and protest against the monster Slavery and the bloody war which is to perpetuate it. I say when a war is declared for the purpose of enslaving and selling American women, I should prove recreant to my duties to God and man, did I not raise my voice in solemn protest against such profligacy."

She predicted that the war would go badly—the Southerners would fear to fight it because they were needed at home to prevent insurrection, and the Northerners, plagued with guilt, would fall ill of pestilence. A defeat would be good, for it would bring an end to the American government as presently constituted, and so to the "slave power."

"Mr. Chairman, although I am a non-resistant," Abby said, "yet I venture to say that this war may be the very best thing that we can have . . . though it may result in the destruction of the Government. Not that the war will bring liberty—no war ever brought liberty . . . but if the land is again to be desolated with war, I ask you will it bring a greater calamity upon the country than that with which she is already burdened? I believe not. I believe with Joshua R. Giddings and John Quincy Adams that war will be the greatest blessing that can befall this people, though to the nation it be a curse. Though it scatter the nation to fragments. But let the nation be accursed so that the people be saved!"

As she reached her peroration, Abby swung her arms and stamped her feet. Smoke seemed to be curling from her very toes. In fact, there was smoke. Suddenly Stephen Foster stepped forward to announce that the platform itself was on fire, and the hall must immediately be vacated. It seemed to many a fitting end to a fiery speech.

Unpopular from the start, the Mexican War was bitterly fought by the abolitionists and others. Whigs gained in the state and congressional elections that fall, and one Senator went to the unprecedented length of voting against war appropriations. Abby and Stephen continued to take the position that war was the inevitable outcome of a corrupt state, and that it should be welcomed rather than denounced since it was sure to bring a total downfall to the government.

This position infuriated many people within and without the antislavery movement. Back in Ohio, they met a stormier opposition than they had ever known before.

In Unionville, a small town near Ashtabula, a young Whig lawyer, J. H. How, began to appear at their meetings to heckle them and insult Abby. Finally, early in July 1846, he brought charges against the Fosters for disturbing the Sabbath by selling books and had a warrant issued for their arrest.

This was old stuff for Stephen. He refused to acknowledge the authority of the arresting constable and declined to produce Abby. The officer then forced his way into their bedroom, where Abby was calmly writing letters.

"Mrs. Foster," he blurted out, "I have got a warrant for you."

Abby turned around and looked him up and down scornfully. "You have got a warrant for me? Who are you?"

"My name is Parker," the man said, visibly losing confidence.

"Well, Mr. Parker, leave my bedroom this instant—you are here on mean, wicked business. Get out of my room, and don't let me see you again."

Parker nearly ran from the room, muttering, "Mrs. Foster says she shan't go with me."

Parker, however, had a writ to serve. An hour later he returned with reinforcements. The deputies seized hold of Stephen, but Abby, rushing to his rescue, threw her arms about his neck and declared, "It may be your business to separate husbands and wives in the South, but you cannot do it here."

With both Abby and Stephen limp and nonresistant, the small group of deputies were unable to push and shove them further than the porch. Fresh recruits were needed to place them in a carriage and take them to the home of Deacon Cunningham, who had preferred the charges.

Here the Fosters would not leave the carriage. When the good deacon came forward and read the charges against them, they would not answer guilty or not guilty. Instead, Abby gave the man a tonguelashing.

"A century ago my Quaker ancestors were acquainted with Deacons in New England," she told him. "Their backs were stripped and whipped until the skin was torn off, their ears were cut off, they were sometimes even put to death for breaking the sabbath and other alleged offenses. I have no doubt you would commit similar barbarities upon my person if you thought public sentiment would allow it."

It being too late to try to continue with the case that night, the bewildered marshal and his deputies next took the Fosters to a tavern, carried their nonresisting bodies to a public room, and left them to sleep while three men guarded their door. It was July, and hot, but according to Stephen they had a refreshing night's sleep. In the morning they were carried to the courthouse, where again they refused to answer charges or defend themselves.

Things might have continued in this manner indefinitely had not a young local lawyer undertaken to defend the Fosters. By crossexamining prosecution witnesses, he managed to prove that the selling of books on the Sabbath was a common practice in the vicinity. In fact, Deacon Cunningham was one of the best salesmen.

In his summation, the young lawyer then used the occasion as an opportunity to make an eloquent antislavery speech. Since many of Abby and Stephen's friends had driven miles to be at the trial, he had an enthusiastic group in the audience.

Immediately upon being set free, the Fosters addressed the crowd, applauded by their friends, and greeted by the yells and groans of their opponents.

Abby thus came away from her act of civil disobedience triumphant, having said just the right thing at the right time, and having been even more scornful than Stephen. She had acted at last in the tradition of her Quaker ancestors, who had refused to pay war taxes, serve in the militia, or obey any law abridging freedom of speech and religion. She had finally followed Stephen in those acts of defiance of the law she so admired. Whatever inhibitions she may have had about breaking the law were now behind her. She was a nonresistant in deed as well as in name.

Just before this exciting experience, Abby had written to Lucy Stone to say that she and Stephen intended to make their return trip to Oberlin. When would be a good time? Lucy and a fellow student, Samuel Creighton, wrote back to advise the Fosters to wait until after the commencement exercises held in early September. Lucy also confided that the Fosters were still under constant attack. The faculty had found that the anti-Sabbath tracts contained misquotations and other careless mistakes, and had pronounced them dishonest. The Fosters were therefore regarded as dishonest for having distributed them.

On the heels of this letter came another from Samuel Creighton, sorrowfully announcing that the faculty had voted against receiving the Fosters and enclosing a note from Lucy. Perhaps unwisely, Lucy repeated all the gossip about the Fosters then circulating on campus.

Abby was furious. "Was I too censorious when at Elyria I impeached the sincerity of the Oberlin faculty?" she asked. "Such people would be beneath contempt were it not that they have souls to save, and that they are doing so much mischief. . . . You believe them sincere 'all but one.' What reasons have you for such a belief? Did they not know our sentiments as well last winter as today? Then why did they not at that time frankly say what they do now? . . . But Satan truly is let loose. And so another fabrication to destroy my influence for saving my sisters from chains and polutions [sic]. My appearance is immodest, and I am bringing offspring into the world to suffer in consequence of my improprieties. *I am no more going to have a baby than you are.* . . . If I am not mistaken in physiological facts, I never can be a mother while I work so hard in this cause. And I must exercise self-denial for the sake of the mothers who are childless."

Among the Oberlin faculty the president alone had spoken in favor of allowing the Fosters to speak, more because of his commitment to freedom of speech than because he agreed with their views. Overriding the faculty vote, he told Samuel Creighton to invite them. He would provide a house and see that they were treated well. Never ones to miss an opportunity or step away from a challenge, the Fosters accepted and arranged to be in Oberlin the second Tuesday of September.

The black citizens of Oberlin, having by this time heard about the ruckus, insisted that the Fosters be allowed to speak in the college chapel. They, a few students, and President Mahan were on hand to listen to the pair when a meeting was held. But the faculty stayed away and refused to retract its violent accusations.

Abby was deeply wounded by this behavior, perhaps because she harbored a respect for learning. Several years later, when Stephen proposed to return, she told him she didn't see how he could contemplate again casting his pearls before such dirty swine.

# XIII

# The Demands of Motherhood

ABBY was, of course, mistaken in her notions of physiology. It was quite possible for her to become pregnant while lecturing. In fact, she did. Almost nine months from the day she wrote Lucy her indignant letter, she gave birth to her only child.

True, however, to her growing concern for women's rights, Abby did not retire until her pregnancy was well advanced. Instead she continued to lecture, remaining in the Ohio area until early winter, and then returning to Massachusetts and New Hampshire. In February, just four months before the baby was born, she was pelted with rotten eggs at Abington, Massachusetts. Appearing in public while pregnant was contrary to the customs of the day, and Abby was criticized afresh for her outlandish behavior.

Late in February, she finally decided the time had come to rest and await the baby's birth. She went to live with the Foster parents in Canterbury, New Hampshire, while Stephen continued to lecture and to look for a farm.

He had been looking off and on since the fall of 1845, but

now his search had a new urgency. Once he had thought of forming a commune in New York State, and again of buying a place in Pennsylvania. Abby talked him out of the commune idea, and he himself decided against Pennsylvania because of its warm summers and high taxes. Stephen himself later in life confessed he was wedded to New England. "I should hate to put my spade into the ground where it did not hit against a rock," he admitted.

In the late winter of 1847 his search narrowed to Massachusetts and the vicinity of Abby's native Worcester. In February he saw a farm there which he liked very much, but it was completely beyond his means. Stephen had been saving his royalties from *The Brotherhood of Thieves* and as much of his salary as an antislavery agent as he could. Abby, though a pennypincher, still felt it wrong to accept a salary herself. She excused Stephen for doing so, since he had to look after their "rainy days."

Finally in April Stephen wrote Abby that he had bought the Cook place, a farm on the western outskirts of Worcester near Abby's childhood home, Tatnuck Hill. An old farmhouse, built in 1797, it was not exactly what Abby had in mind, and with her usual frankness she let him know it:

"How idle it is to lay plans," she wrote. "The very reverse of ours, in relation to a house, is realized."

She enumerated her grievances. They had wanted only a few acres, but Stephen had bought a great many. They had wanted first-rate soil, but this was third- or fourth-rate. They had wanted to grow fruit, but the soil would be too poor. They had decided to look for a place with buildings that were either very good, or poor enough to tear down. The buildings on the Cook place fitted neither description. They had wanted to be in town, but this was three or four miles out. Moreover, Stephen was talking as though there would be more than one family in the house.

"But I presume you have done the best you could under the circumstances," she concluded ". . . you will not find me a grumbler, although my air castles are all demolished with one blow. I am too much of a philosopher to take any such disappointment to heart, but think it best to go to work and make the best of things."

With one more parting shot—Tatnuck was full of bigots and therefore a neighborhood repulsive to her—Abby turned to outlining her plans for getting the place in shape. She had hired Alvida Ballou, her brother-in-law's sister, to give her a hand. She would go to her younger sister Lucy's wedding and then come to Tatnuck Hill with Alvida to get to work making it decent. Stephen had better not buy anything for the house meanwhile since she was, as he knew, "an old maid." Stephen in fact ought to come to the wedding and meet more of the Kelley tribe, although she hoped he would buy a new coat and vest before he came.

The farmhouse of which Abby so bitterly complained was actually a large, handsome red-brick structure, built in the Georgian style, with two chimneys and a fanlight over the front door. It was run-down, however. She would probably have preferred a new house, built in the Greek revival style then popular throughout New England.

Stephen's plan was to operate the farm in partnership with his brother Galen, and to ask his younger brother, Newell, to farm it while Stephen continued to earn a salary as an antislavery agent. They would all live together for a while. Abby remonstrated. She did not want to share the house; why not tear down the old kitchen and build a new wing for the other family? At any rate she wanted to get the place into decent shape so that her old friend, Paulina Wright, recently widowed, could be with her at the time of the birth of her child. "I do not want a doctor," she declared emphatically.

Alla was born May 17, 1847. Abby was thirty-six. She was used to being independent and feared being tied down. Now, however, she threw herself into motherhood enthusiastically, devoting most of her energies to the care of her infant. Interested in the values of hydrotherapy, or "water cure," then becoming popular with reformers, she plunged little Alla into a cold bath every morning from the age of six weeks on. The baby did not cry, she reported, only looked surprised. She took her outside as often as possible, and when she left her alone on the bed she dropped the *Anti-Slavery Bugle* beside her, so that her daughter might start out under the proper influences.

For his part, Stephen threw himself just as energetically into getting the new farm in order. The fields were low and waterlogged. They had to be drained, the pond emptied of mud, the orchard spread with manure. There was no barn. In June his brother Galen arrived from Erie, Pennsylvania, to help put the farm in shape, and a week later his younger brother, Newell, with his wife, Eliza, numerous children, and several hired men. Soon various members of the Foster and Kelley families started coming for overnight visits, and Stephen's aged parents came for a long visit. The old farmhouse was full to overflowing.

Abby found she did not like this confused household. She herself was a meticulous housewife. She wanted, she told Alla years later, to prove that a strong-minded woman could be an excellent housekeeper. Her sister-in-law was far more careless, and Abby was upset when her furniture was mishandled.

Stoically, she said nothing of this to Stephen at first, and Stephen went off to his lecturing in August, leaving Abby as a boarder in the household, sure that she would be well cared for. Then she wrote him about it:

"I never want to keep house again till we can live less mixed up. . . . I have an increasing dislike of this mixture. I am happy and try to make those about me comfortable but we should all be better satisfied to have our own bird's nest separate."

Wrapped up though she was in the baby, Abby found she missed her husband terribly. "My thoughts are too much with thee—I fear I love the creature more than the creator," she wrote him in September.

Traveling with Garrison, Douglass, and Lucy Stone, holding large and successful meetings, Stephen had less time to pine. Still, he missed Abby. When urged by the American Society to "take the field" in New York State that winter, he wrote urging her to join him. They would be as they were before; the absence of the baby would leave no vacuum.

Abby could not agree. "She has so thoroughly entwined herself about me that I fear it would rend me to pieces to take her away. It is not to be expected you can feel as I do. You have not been with her constantly for nearly four months, and watched her every look and heard her every breath; seen intelligence dawning upon her and expanding by every hour. She does not look up to you as to me, so imploringly for food and the supplying of all her wants, reminding me constantly of her utter dependence and of her incapacity to defend herself from the wrongs she might suffer, that I am her natural guardian and under the most sacred obligation to make her happy. Yes, for me, there must always be a vacuum where our little one is not. The love I bear her is trifling compared with that which I bear her father, but I should feel her absence much."

It might be possible for her to come to New York State with the baby for the winter, she thought, but then again it would be more expensive than staying where she was. She didn't like being in debt, and it would cost her more to board with another family, and would mean buying new clothes for herself and the baby. No, she would stay where she was and put up with the confusion.

After her exciting life to date, she had to admit domesticity was dull. In fact, as she wrote a friend a year or so later, "It was perfectly killing." The arrival of a neighbor was an event worth recording. Letters from Stephen bringing her news of the beloved cause were manna from heaven. So were the antislavery newspapers when they arrived. She wrote to her friend Sydney Gay to ask for a subscription to the *Standard* and peppered Stephen with questions about her beloved *Anti-Slavery Bugle*.

Both the *Bugle* and the *Standard* were in precarious positions that fall. Without a word to the Garrisonians, Frederick Douglass had begun to publish at Rochester yet another antislavery paper, *The North Star*. It was the first such paper to be published by a black for the blacks and therefore filled a real void, but at the same time it threatened the life of the little *Bugle*, which tried to cover much the same territory. Abby had always distrusted Douglass. She felt that his paper came at a terrible time, when the campaign in New York

State was going badly, and no distinction seemed to be made between Old Organization, New Organization, and Liberty party. It probably added to Abby's impatience that she was stuck at home when she was needed to renew the fire.

Fortunately, Worcester was an abolitionist stronghold, and there were many interesting antislavery events to attend. Abby had difficulty arranging to make the three-mile trip to town, but she contrived it in August when Lucretia Mott, Charles Burleigh, and William Brown came to lecture. Somehow Abby had never managed to hear Lucretia say more than a few words at an antislavery meeting. Now she took her baby into town to spend the weekend so as not to miss a syllable. She was delighted by her fellow Quaker's speech. Lucretia said that Christianity ought to be expressed in deeds, not empty forms, and she endorsed all reforms "from that of laying aside the whip stick in families to that of thorough non-resistance, temperance, antislavery, women's rights, moral reform." "I think her decidedly more radical than when I saw her last," Abby concluded.

Between Stephen's urgings, Lucretia's inspiration, and her own boredom, Abby decided that she would wean Alla early and return to antislavery lecturing the next year. Caroline, Stephen's younger sister, was willing to take care of the baby in Abby's absence. A gentle schoolteacher, she was just the sort of person to whom Abby felt she would be able to entrust her precious child.

"Stephen says I shall not be willing to leave her," Abby wrote the Gays. "We shall see whether I care so much for my baby as to forget the multitudes of broken-hearted mothers."

It was an unpopular decision. Even her good friend and fellow abolitionist Lizzie Jones demurred. "For the sake of the slave I am glad you are going to lecture next March, but for the sake of millions of suffering children whose mothers have thrown off the duties and responsibilities of mothers and left them in the care of aunts and sisters and hired nurses who cannot have for them the feelings of a parent, I am sorry," she wrote. "Your example will strengthen this too prevalent custom. Your influence on the course of human freedom will be good but your influence on home duties and home virtues will be bad. If you would wait until your child is old enough to wean it might be less reprehensible. I shall set a better example whether anyone follows it or not. If the little stranger that we now expect to come to bless us in less than six months shall live I think I shall not feel like leaving it, to lecture, in ten months."

Abby was, as usual, sensitive to criticism, and often defended herself for leaving Alla. Her baby had the best of care, she insisted, while the slave mother's had none at all. Deeply concerned for Alla's health and happiness, she wrote Caroline an anxious stream of questions and advice about the child whenever she was away. Yet Abby was determined not to give up until the slave obtained his freedom. It turned out to be a long, long haul.

Though her work was both her duty and her joy, Abby continued to hate being separated from Stephen and Alla. Sometimes Stephen joined her for meetings, and they spent one winter together lecturing in Michigan. Most of the time, though, he was home in Worcester, working on their farm. "It is terrible this going about alone, warming up people's spare beds," she complained.

Being away from Alla was worse in a way, because it conflicted with her sense of duty. "I feel that it is a great sacrifice indeed for me to be away from Alla at this interesting period of her intellectual, moral, and social development," she wrote Stephen. "Children are like daguerreotype plates—they catch the images that are thrown upon them. The preaching and teaching does but little, tis the passing life that affects them most."

In order to compensate for her absence, Abby wrote Alla a constant stream of letters describing her adventures, admonishing Alla to be a good girl, obey her aunts, and think often about the poor slaves. Alla dictated letters back and began printing her own when she was five or six.

Abby found she missed the daily life of the farm, as she traveled, and often begged for more details. The one who is at home has more interesting letters to write than the one who is away, she wrote Stephen. There was a certain sameness to the life of a lecturer, but it was around the affairs of the home that "the affections cluster."

Because they took turns traveling, Stephen became more interested in the education of little Alla than most fathers of that day. Several times when Abby urged him to join her in lecturing, he wrote back that he didn't think it wise to leave his daughter when she had just been ill, was lonely, or seemed to be at an important stage of development.

Abby for her part began to take more and more of an interest in farming. Although she had originally hated the Cook place, she began to be quite fond of it. Eventually, Stephen added a wing and some sheds and outhouses, which they both agreed were an improvement. After that, they thought less and less about moving someplace else. Abby began to inquire in her letters about the progress of the orchard and the crops, and to send Stephen literature on fruit

nurture. Stephen once told her he didn't have much confidence in her as a farmer. Nevertheless, when he was away
she increasingly took over the farm management. She
sometimes wore the new bloomer costume for women when
she worked around the farm, though passersby stared.

Probably because they were both away so much, the farm
operated at a loss for most of its early years. Stephen had
trouble getting help, and even his hard-working brother
Adam, who came to manage the farm for a while, didn't
always accomplish as much as he would like to see done. As a
result, the Fosters were in debt, and forced to borrow, on and
off, for many years. Abby hated it. All her life she had been a
pennypincher, but Stephen—probably because he was so
worried—sometimes accused her of being careless with
money.

Stephen did not learn to sew, or Abby to plough, but the
two came much closer than any other couple of that period to
interchanging duties. They did it because it was practical and
because it helped them serve the cause to which their lives
were devoted. Poverty, ill health, and separation caused many
strains. Yet it was a good marriage, described by a neighbor as
one in which "two of the very strongest individualities united
in one absolutely independent and perfectly harmonious
union."

Stephen, and perhaps Abby too, was disappointed there
were no more children. Once Stephen wrote to Abby
describing how Alla had climbed onto his knee and said he
was a poor man because he had only one little daughter. "Do
you think you will ever make me a rich man by her
definition?" he asked a bit plaintively.

For leaving her husband and baby for the sake of the cause,

Abby was an inspiration to many other women. One housewife in Ohio wrote a long, earnest poem, comparing her to the early missionaries:

But thou, with courage more heroic yet
　　Hast braved the torrent of abuse and scorning;
Colder and sterner spirits thou hast met,
　　Than she amid the heathen lands of morning.

O, faithful-hearted! thou hast given up *all*—
　　All the sweet joys that cluster round Home's altar,
And given thy life for those in captive thrall,
　　With a devotion that will never falter.

Forth from the ark of happiness and love,
　　Stifling the feelings of a wife and mother,
Thou journeyest like the Patriarch's faithful dove,
　　In pity for the sorrows of another:

Pleading for her condemned in chains to mourn,
　　Driven to her unpaid labors, scourged and gory,
Whose helpless babes are from her bosom torn,
　　Beneath our country's stars and stripes of glory!

Thou askest no reward, but it will come!
　　The wreath of amaranth shall yet be given,
When thou at last shalt reach a peaceful home,
　　Upon the bright and stormless shore of Heaven.

# XIV

# *Back on the Campaign Trail*

BY spring 1848, Alla was weaned and Abby was ready to venture forth again. Late in March she set off for New York and Philadelphia to try to raise money for the *Bugle*. She got along comfortably, taking care of herself and her own luggage and enjoyed being "just as *outlandish* as it happens to be convenient, no one saying 'why do you so?' "

"I have discovered the cause of my *lawlessness*, as you seem to consider it, in my manner among folks," she wrote Stephen. "It consists in the fact of my feeling that I am as much unobserved as if I were entirely alone. I don't feel the presence of the multitudes, even when I am crowding among them—they are nothing to my feeling—no more than so many images in a museum. I find, on looking into my inner man, that this has always been the fact with me. I feel the presence only of those whom I intimately know."

Feeling free as a bird, her thoughts still centered on Alla. In New York she consulted a famous clairvoyant, who conjured up an image of the baby and told Abby that Alla was suffering from worms. Abby trustingly bought some bottles of a herbal medicine prescribed by the clairvoyant's manager and had them sent to Caroline Foster with whom Alla was staying.

From New York, Abby went on to Philadelphia, then to Long Island, where she held some meetings. Then it was time to go to the anniversary meetings of the American Anti-Slavery Society, held in New York as usual in May. This year the abolitionists could rejoice that the war with Mexico was at last ended, thanks in part to their principled opposition. On the other hand, the question of the extension of slavery into the huge new territories acquired from Mexico was not settled. It was no time to sit back on their laurels.

Abby was among those urging renewed efforts. She reminded her listeners of the "degradation and servile condition of black women, how they are exposed to the licentious brutality of their task masters, how they are whipped and chained and polluted. Would not anyone of you do anything in his power to get rid of such a state of things?" she appealed.

After this successful return to public life, Abby spent most of the summer and fall home in Worcester with Alla, while Stephen toured Massachusetts. From her little writing-desk in the front parlor, Abby kept in touch with her husband and antislavery friends and did what she could to prepare for the antislavery fairs.

These fairs, held annually, had become one of the chief sources of funds for the antislavery cause. All over the North women met in sewing circles all year long to prepare articles of clothing or household use to be sold at the fairs. Abby had originally objected to the custom—the fact that raffles were often held in connection with the fairs went against her

Quaker principles—and she later felt she had no knack for the merchandising. Still, she organized sewing circles, and sewed herself for the cause. The fact that her great friend Maria Chapman played a major role in organizing the antislavery fairs was a powerful inducement to Abby to participate.

While Abby wrote letters, and Stephen lectured, the rest of the nation was caught up in the excitement of another presidential election. The matter most debated was the Wilmot Proviso, forbidding the extension of slavery into the newly acquired territories. Those opposed to it called for "squatters' rights," the right of the inhabitants of the states-to-be to make their own decisions. When both the Whigs and the Democrats nominated men pledged to squatters' rights, the antislavery Whigs and Democrats joined with former members of the Liberty party to form the Free Soil party. Martin Van Buren was nominated for President and a slogan adopted calling for "Free soil, free speech, free labor, and free men."

Abby and Stephen found themselves trapped in the same old dilemma. While feeling some attraction to the Free Soilers, they continued to believe that politics was the opiate of the people, that it took their minds off more fundamental things. As more and more abolitionists turned in their frustration to political action, the campaign would again suffer. No, the Fosters felt, they must once more take the field to fight the Free Soil party as they had fought the Liberty party. They would return to their beloved New York State to renew the battle.

Their first major campaign was planned for Long Island in the summer of 1849. Abby and Stephen decided to announce only the first meeting, relying on growing interest to bring their audience back to a second and a third. This technique, borrowed from the revivalists, was one they used with increasing frequency.

Interest on Long Island was immediate—and violent. They spoke first on a Sunday in Flushing, Long Island, under the famous oak tree where George Fox, the founder of Quakerism, had first preached to the inhabitants. Abby had hardly begun when hecklers interrupted, accusing her of desecrating the Sabbath. Abby flashed a haughty glance but continued with her lecture. Next came a shower of rotten eggs. Somehow, through all the years of peltings, Abby had never once been hit. This time an egg landed on her skirt, broke, and revealed a full-grown chick inside.

"It saved me having to clean my dress," Abby later remarked wryly.

Eggs or no, the Fosters continued until they had completed their meetings. Abby had been spared the animosity of the crowd for almost two years and found it more upsetting now than before.

Characteristically, however, she tried to understand the cause. It was because a large number of landed proprietors owned all the property here, she reasoned, and the great mass of people were wholly dependent upon them. In this "servile condition," how could the common man or woman be expected to have a spirit of free inquiry? She began to wonder more and more if the concentration of economic power had something to do with the deplorable state of the nation.

From Long Island the Fosters moved on to the Hudson River Valley, where they spent the summer and fall in Dutchess and Ulster counties, converting a local pastor to comeouterism, and organizing giant antislavery rallies and picnics. To aid her campaign, Abby arranged for the famous Hutchison family, who sang antislavery songs, to be present as often as possible. She also tried to persuade Isaac Hopper, a venerable and beloved abolitionist, to attend. No matter where she was, Abby always felt that was the most important field to cultivate. From Wappingers Falls and Milton, she sent a stream of letters to her fellow abolitionists urging them to come immediately, to send help, to plan an extended campaign.

In the course of 1849 Abby began to receive a salary from the American Anti-Slavery Society. She was given the title of general agent and organizer of regional campaigns. Abby was eager that Stephen apply for the same position, but he felt more and more that he was not fitted for the work.

"I have often told you that you could accomplish more alone than with my aid," Stephen wrote to her in the spring of 1850, after she had raised some money on a solo mission. "So you have additional evidence not only that I am not fitted for general agent, but that I am not fit even for a lecturing agent. Of this I have long been conscious, and now I hope and trust you will not again urge me into the field. I can labor, but I do not think either writing or public speaking is my proving. I need not tell you that I have a strong and growing dislike of both."

Stephen had gradually been losing his enthusiasm for lecturing ever since he fell in love with Abby. He genuinely admired her more reasoned and polished arguments and began to be less sure of himself in his thundering denunciations. His many critics claimed he was only happy playing the martyr or "Saint Stephen." He clearly enjoyed hostile crowds. Abby didn't, and persuaded him that it was no longer their duty to speak to disturbed meetings.

"Liberty of speech has now been regained throughout the North except in some benighted corners," she concluded.

For Abby's sake, Stephen made several more lecturing tours, but his heart was no longer in it. "You can hardly imagine what a dislike I have to this wandering mode of life," he wrote once. "It is the next thing to being a slave. But it is no use complaining to you, as with you it is the only way in which we can be of use in the world."

By the spring of 1850 he was adamant. He had just bought a load of young fruit trees and hired additional help to raise a new barn. He was needed at Worcester. Abby must go alone to Ohio where they had next been called.

Reluctantly she did so, taking a Lake Erie steamer. Just to be safe, she bought a life preserver. Her beloved Buckeyes received her enthusiastically. Wherever she went, she drew large crowds, sometimes three thousand strong. In the southern part of the state there had been so much slander circulated against her that she had "a most suffering time." Yet even here she felt she was gaining ground, and was able to raise a great deal of money, going from house to house.

Everyone asked for Stephen, she reported tactfully in letters home, and he was badly needed. Parker Pillsbury was supposed to join her, but he had become ill. Could not Stephen come and take his place? She was never able to lay out the subject of the sinfulness of church attendance as Stephen could.

When Parker recovered and came west, Abby developed a new strategy to get Stephen active again. Would he not meet her in Syracuse on her way home? They could then proceed back to Worcester together, lecturing here and there. If she were to be general agent, she must know the lay of the land. Gerrit Smith, their old friend and adversary, had given money to the American Society for the first time in several years. Stephen was the very man to capitalize on this, and help Gerrit see the true light.

Stephen wrote that he would consider the idea but that meanwhile he had decided to lecture on antislavery every Sunday in the Worcester vicinity. Feeling the crowds to be too lukewarm and apathetic at these meetings, he shocked one audience by announcing that he was going to return to his old ways of interrupting church services. None of this, he wrote Abby, held a candle to her labors.

"Your great success, however, throws me entirely into the shade, and might awaken my envy, if it were not, after all, my own. As it is, I can only congratulate myself on this exercise of that good sense and sound discrimination which made you my first choice among all the women of my acquaintance, and the good fortune which placed such a prize within my grasp."

When Abby accused him of flattery, he responded with his most eloquent love letter to date. "You accuse me of flattery, and of acting the part of a lover, a character in which I made but a sorry figure, as you think, during our courtship. To the first of these charges I plead, 'Not guilty.' The latter is possibly true as I never felt more like a lover than at the present time . . . my early love was the spring of hope, my present the fruit of knowledge. My lady love was an insubstantial personage, changing with every successive change in the phase of my fancy. . . . My wife is a real entity. I know *what* I love, and *why*."

While Abby went on to success after success in Ohio, Stephen dealt with a series of small crises in Worcester. The carpenters who built his barn framed it so badly that it would not come together and had to be done over again. It rained during the barnraising and again at haying time. Two sisters-in-law quarreled over disciplining little Alla. His younger brother, Adam, was taken ill with a "cramp of the bowel" (probably appendicitis) and was near death when a doctor of hydrotherapy prescribed for him. He was to be immersed in ice-cold water, wrapped in cold sheets, and given constant enemas. Stephen nursed Adam himself, while the whole family ran to and from the spring, and miraculously, he recovered.

All these occurrences delayed Stephen's farming. He finally decided he could not get away to meet Abby. Instead she made the New York State tour alone, stopping to speak at several antislavery gatherings.

The abolitionists in New York State and elsewhere were agitated and depressed in the early fall of 1850. Following a great debate between Daniel Webster and Henry Clay on the admission of the new territories won from Mexico, the Congress was passing piece by piece the legislation that made up the Compromise of 1850.

California was to be admitted to the Union as a free state; Utah and New Mexico would be given a choice between being slave or free when they were admitted; the slave trade would be abolished in the District of Columbia, but not slavery itself. Most ominous of all, a new Fugitive Slave Law was passed to take the place of the old law of 1793, still on the books.

The new law levied a thousand dollar fine and six months

in jail on any person who attempted to assist a refugee, and authorized marshals to demand the help of any bystander in the recapture of the slave. There were other provisions, all favorable to the slaveholder and detrimental to the slave.

This was no compromise, the abolitionists assured each other. This was a naked sellout to the slave power. The law was so unfair and so brutal that no man or woman of good conscience could obey it. It must be met by civil disobedience.

For the next decade, Abby was to express her defiance of the law in words and deeds. When it was first passed in September she was angry but not surprised. Speaking in Minerva Hall, in Rochester, she gave her most radical analysis to date of the basis of the slave power:

> While there are fifteen hundred millions of dollars invested in slave property—while it is constitutionally represented on the floor of Congress, and while men are required to swear to support that Constitution, slavery will continue to give laws to the Republic, and it is beyond the power of men or angels to prevent it.
>
> It is a great mistake to suppose that numbers rule in this or any other government. Capital has always ruled, and must, in the nature of things, continue to do so. Capital controls labor; and that which controls the labor of a country will control the government of that country.

The speech, though "ultra," was well-received. A young admirer, Aaron Powell, described Abby as being at her prime, at the very peak of her powers of oratory in the summer of 1850, and her ability to sway audiences was immense. After a long summer of swaying them, however, she was tired and glad to be going home. She reached Worcester in early October, and had a week to rest and enjoy her family before the next major event in her life.

# XV

# *The Rights of Women*

THROUGHOUT the 1840s Abby had been a heroine to all women interested in asserting their rights. Others talked about it; she did it. And because she continued to act on the assumption that she was in fact the equal of any man, she drew down upon her head the wrath of the press, the pulpit, and established society.

If Abby had been tough-skinned she might have seemed less courageous to her contemporaries. But her close friends all knew that she was in fact easily wounded. She worried about her reputation, and her eyes would fill with tears when she repeated some of the things that were said about her. To go ahead in the face of this painful abuse seemed saintlike to her admirers.

But though she was the symbol of women's rights, she herself was too busy with the abolitionist cause to play a prominent role in the development of the women's rights movement. She was devoted to rights of all humans—women, blacks, poor people—but her first priority was the freeing of the slave. She had pledged herself to keep at it until the day of Jubilee, and nothing could swerve her.

She was, therefore, not among the women who organized the Seneca Falls Convention in July 1848, though most of her close friends were present. Set up by Lucretia Mott and Elizabeth Cady Stanton, the convention adopted a group of resolutions setting out for the first time the rights of women.

A sequel to Seneca Falls was the first national women's rights convention, held in Worcester in October 1850, shortly after Abby got home from her Western tour. Abby had been part of the group that had met in May to conceive and plan the convention, but she had been too busy to take a hand in the final arrangements. Instead her great friend Paulina Wright (now remarried, and known as Paulina Wright Davis) had taken on the burden of the work.

Abby's role in this first convention was, therefore, minor, though she was placed on several of the important committees, and made a brief speech.

Instead it was Stephen, himself an ardent feminist, who gave one of the major addresses. Christ himself believed in the equality of women, Stephen asserted; He would have had no dealing with the Old Testament prophets who thought otherwise.

Next year, however, it was Abby's turn. At the second women's rights convention, in the fall of 1851, also held in Worcester, she presented a resolution that startled and appalled many in her audience:

> Resolved . . . That woman lacks her rights, because she does not feel the full weight of her responsibilities; that when she shall feel her responsibilities

sufficiently to induce her to go forward and discharge
them, she will inevitably obtain her rights; when she
shall feel herself equally bound with her father,
husband, brother and son, to provide for the physical
necessities and elegances of life, when she shall feel
as deep responsibility as they for the intellectual and
moral and religious elevation of the race, she will of
necessity seek out and enter those paths of Physical,
Intellectual, Moral and Religious Labor which are
necessary for the accomplishment of her object. Let
her feel the full stimulus of motive and she will
achieve the means.

Girls ought to be raised to believe that they should be able
to provide for a family before they got married, Abby insisted.
Since the traditional pursuits open to women were crowded,
they must seek out other ways to make a living.

Nor, Abby said, to the increasingly startled audience, was it
all man's fault.

Society says, keep your daughters, like dolls in the
parlor; they must not do anything to aid in
supporting the family. . . . If we could look under
and within the broadcloth and velvet, we should find
as many breaking hearts, and as many sighs and
groans, and as much mental anguish, as we find in
the parlor, as we find in the nursery in any house in
Worcester. But woman is vain and frivolous, and
man is ignorant and therefore, he is what he is . . . a
mere machine for calculating and getting money.

My friends, I feel that in throwing out this idea, I
have done what was left for me to do. But I did not
rise to make a speech. For fourteen years I have

advocated this cause in my daily life. Bloody feet, sisters, have worn smooth the path by which you have come hither. You will not need to speak when you speak by your everyday life. Action is eloquence. Let us then, when we go home, go not to complain, but to work. . . .

There are thousands of women in these United States working for a starving pittance, who know and feel that they are fitted for something better, and who tell me when I talk with them, and urge them to open shops and do business for themselves, "I do not want the responsibility of business, it is too much." Well, then starve in your laziness.

She did not speak in anger, Abby said (although it may have sounded so); she simply felt that women had been throwing too much of the blame to the men. "We have been groping about in the dark. We are trying to find our way, and God give us light."

No applause greeted these remarks. Abby was attacking the very dynamic of the early women's rights movement: its anger against men. Most of the women in the hall needed to be angry in order to make the transition to which Abby was calling them, and which she had herself already made.

This speech may have cost Abby the leadership she deserved in the movement she helped to inspire. Undeterred by her unpopularity, however, she continued to attend and to speak at the women's rights conventions for the next several years. If she gave the women's movement less and less time it was because she was increasingly caught up with the agitation against the Fugitive Slave Law. Not until after the Civil War did she feel able to make feminism a first priority.

All through the years she continued nevertheless to be an inspiration to the women who led the movement. She stayed in Seneca Falls with Elizabeth Cady Stanton, who often referred to her in her memoirs as an inspiring influence. Lecturing against slavery in 1851, she had as a traveling companion a young Quaker called Susan B. Anthony, who was to become a famous feminist. Later Susan visited Abby at the farm in Tatnuck Hill.

Abby was as enthusiastic about finding Susan as she had been years ago about finding Lucy Stone: "I think she had grown intellectually more than any other person of my acquaintance," she wrote a friend.

Several years later Abby and Susan together attended the World Temperance Convention, held in New York City, in May of 1853. When they tried to speak from the floor, they were ordered to take their seats by the presiding officer, a clergyman.

Abby tried to point out that it couldn't be called the World Temperance Convention if it excluded half of the world—that is, women—from its deliberations, but she was shouted down.

She and Susan therefore led a group of feminists—male and female—from the building. On the steps outside they decided to hold a Whole World's Temperance Convention that fall.

Inside the hall, meanwhile, the chairman congratulated the gathering on being able to proceed, now that the "scum of the convention has left."

Actions like these won her the devotion of Lucy Stone, Susan Anthony, Elizabeth Stanton, Lucretia Mott, Paulina Wright Davis, and other leaders of the women's movement. Among the rank and file, however, there was fear that her "odious reputation" might damage their cause. There is one report that at a women's rights convention she was denied a seat on the platform because of her notoriety.

In 1856 the Reverend Theodore Parker preached a sermon which was reprinted in *The Liberator*, describing and condemning such an incident:

> Here is a woman in Massachusetts who has travelled all over the North, laboring for woman's Cause. She bore the burden and heat of the day. She was an outcast from society. Other women hated her; men insulted her. . . . The noble woman bore it with no complaint; only now and then in private, the great heart of Abby Kelley would fill her eyes with tears at the thought of this injustice. . . . But when the cause had won something of respect, a great Convention of women and the friends of women was summoned to meet in the heart of this commonwealth and those who had control of the matter thought it would not do to have woman's stoutest champion to sit upon the platform. She must sit below it, lest it hurt the cause and peril the rights of women to have woman's noblest champion sit in woman's honored place!

# XVI

# To Aid the Fugitive

FOR many years Northern abolitionists had found one practical way to express their abhorrence of slavery. They had helped escaping slaves make their way from the Mason-Dixon line across the Northern states to Canada and safety.

Traveling at night, led at times only by the North Star, hiding in barns and cellars of abolitionists by day, the blacks escaped in increasing numbers. They were aided by a network of free blacks and abolitionists in the North, who passed them on from one place of safety to the next, right under the noses of the slavecatchers. The Underground Railroad was the name given to this escape route.

Naturally the Foster farm became a station on the Underground Railroad soon after Abby and Stephen bought it. In their cellar was a secret vault, five feet by ten feet in size, which could only be reached by a trap door from the room above. So many escaping slaves stayed in that cellar that the old Cook place began to be known as Liberty Farm.

Now the operation of the whole Underground Railroad was threatened by the Fugitive Slave Law of 1850, which increased the fines of those caught assisting the refugees and added to the rewards of those catching them.

The only way to fight this harsh law was to preach civil disobedience. "We must all be ready to sacrifice our lives, and to make this sacrifice today, if need be, for the cause of freedom," Abby cried passionately at an antislavery meeting in Rochester. "No fugitive slave shall be taken from this city if throwing my body in the path of the kidnappers, and sacrificing my life, can prevent it." The abolitionists, however, should not use force, other than moral force, she argued. Only the right means would obtain the right ends.

Stephen was less sure. He thought perhaps it was right to advocate that the escaping slaves defend themselves with force of arms. Citizens who were not pacifists ought also to use arms to prevent the slaves' recapture. In fact, the Southern slaves ought to rise in bloody rebellion. With him, he now declared, nonresistance was only a technique, not a principle.

A series of dramatic efforts by the blacks, some aided by the abolitionists, to rescue escaped slaves from the hands of the federal marshals, took place in the months directly following the passage of the Fugitive Slave Law. The Fosters read about them avidly in the antislavery press and longed for an opportunity to prove themselves in action.

In February 1851 the ex-slave Frederick Jenkins, nicknamed Shadrach, was rescued in Boston from the hands of the law when a crowd of blacks burst into the courtroom and carried off the prisoner. Before the officers had recovered from their surprise, he was on his way to Canada. In April, a similar attempt to rescue an escaped slave called Thomas Sims failed, and the Boston abolitionists who had tried to assist, mourned their ineffectiveness.

In September, a group of blacks led by a courageous ex-slave, William Parker, thwarted the efforts of a slave-owner, his relatives, and a U.S. marshal to arrest four escaped slaves in Christiana, Pennsylvania. Three bystanders, two of them Quakers, were ordered by the excited marshal to assist. When they refused to do so they were arrested, and eventually brought to trial for treason. For a while, the eyes of the nation, North and South, were focused on the treason trials. Because the charges were so exaggerated, they were eventually dismissed.

Still another exciting rescue took place in Syracuse in October 1851, when a group of abolitionists, including Gerrit Smith and Samuel May, joined with local blacks in releasing a slave nicknamed Jerry from the police station and sending him on to Canada.

The most famous of the rescue attempts occurred in Boston in May 1854. Anthony Burns, an ex-slave, was arrested on a charge of breaking into and robbing a jewelry store. The charge was a pretense; it was simply a way of getting him into the hands of the local police. Hustled off to court, he was confronted with the real problem, his ex-owner. By proving that the arrest was originally illegal, his lawyers persuaded the court to postpone the case for several days. This gave the abolitionists a chance to plan their strategy.

It was decided to hold a mass meeting of abolitionists in Faneuil Hall on Friday night, drawing attention away from the courthouse. During the meeting, a group of blacks were to assault the courthouse, and the abolitionists would join them en masse.

The meeting was held, an announcement made toward the end of it that all were needed at the courthouse, but the rescue attempt itself failed. The attackers were unable to batter down the door or gain entry through the windows, though a guard was killed in the rush.

Thomas Wentworth Higginson, a neighbor of the Fosters, had participated in the rescue attempt. When news of its failure reached Worcester, Stephen took the lead in organizing a mass demonstration of Worcester men in the state capital. A special train took them to Boston, where they were joined by similar delegations from other parts of the Massachusetts countryside.

Despite the size of the crowd, there was no second rescue attempt, and the courtroom procedures continued, the judge finally ruling in favor of the slaveholder. With the help of federal troops, rushed into Boston by President Franklin Pierce, the crowd was held back, and Burns was marched down to the wharf and aboard a ship bound south.

Boston expressed its displeasure. Stores were closed, buildings draped in black, and a coffin suspended from the building at the corner of Washington and State Streets. As Burns marched on his way back to slavery, the crowd cheered him on, booing and hissing his captors.

The Burns case made Stephen increasingly restive under his nonresistance principles. At the May 1854 New England Anti-Slavery Convention, he moved that it appoint a Committee of Vigilance to assist escaping slaves. "Let each fight against slavery with his own weapons," he declared, "violent or nonviolent. But let him fight."

This was, in fact, a time of great testing for the pacifist abolitionists. Should they preach nonresistance to the blacks? Obviously not, for when the slave-owners arrived hot on their trail they were armed to the teeth. But then, at what point did support for the resistance of the blacks compromise their own principles?

The passage of the Kansas-Nebraska Act at the end of May brought the issue into still sharper focus. By permitting both Kansas and Nebraska to decide about slavery on the basis of squatters' rights, Congress repealed the Missouri Compromise and opened both fledgling states to bitter battles between proslavery and antislavery forces. Shortly, both the friends and foes of slavery were encouraging settlers to move to Bleeding Kansas and arming them to the teeth.

Abby objected on nonresistant grounds. She aired her views in a letter to Garrison: "I want those who have been thinking to establish freedom in Kansas by Sharp's rifles to see that if one tithe of the indignation and money that has been expended against border ruffians in Kansas had been used to create a just moral indignation against those around us who sustain those ruffians that Kansas would be free."

As a result of the Anthony Burns case and the Kansas-Nebraska Act, frustration ran high during the summer of 1854 among all the abolitionists. On July 4 William Lloyd Garrison expressed their feeling in a symbolic act. At a meeting in Framingham, Massachusetts, he held aloft a copy of the Fugitive Slave Law, struck a match, and burned it to ashes. Next he burned a copy of the decision in the Burns case. Then came the Constitution of the United States. Calling it "a covenant with death, and an agreement with hell," he put it to the match. "So perish all compromises with tyranny!" he shouted. Abby and Stephen applauded him wildly along with the rest.

In October of that year, when the leaves were turning, Stephen's chance to prove himself finally came. Asa Butman, a notorious slave-kidnapper, came to Worcester. No one knew whether he was there to try to capture an escaped slave, or to gather evidence against those who had tried to rescue Burns in Boston. The free blacks, many of whom belonged to a Vigilance Committee, were made nervous by his presence. They issued a handbill warning others of his presence and announced they were planning to tar and feather him.

Here was a chance to see if nonresistance would work, Stephen thought. He and a few other nonresisters formed a committee to keep Butman under constant surveillance. They stayed up all night, along with members of the Vigilance Committee, guarding the hotel where Butman was staying.

Around 3:00 A.M. Butman, disturbed by the noise, came to the door of his room brandishing a pistol, and was promptly arrested for carrying a concealed weapon. In the morning, when Butman was brought to court, a huge mob had formed outside. Six or seven blacks burst into the courtroom, and one of them struck Butman a heavy blow on the head. Growing alarmed, the marshal locked Butman into his office, along with his assailant, and appealed to the abolitionists to quiet the mob outside.

In response, someone went to find George Hoar, a local lawyer. Hoar's father, Samuel Hoar, had been sent to Charleston in 1844 by the State of Massachusetts to test the law under which South Carolina was jailing all black seamen—including free blacks from Massachusetts—whenever they arrived in her ports. Both the South Carolina state legislature and the press treated Hoar's arrival as an insult and he and his daughter were very nearly lynched.

George Hoar, now standing on the Worcester courthouse steps, reminded his fellow citizens that it was a group of conscientious men of Charleston who had saved his father and his sister from the mob. He then appealed to the honor of the citizens of Worcester to do the same for the unpopular slavecatcher.

It was a moving argument. In response, Stephen and two other abolitionists stepped forward and offered to escort Butman to the train station. Stephen thus got a chance to try his theories of nonresistance against the furious mob.

"I threw myself into his rear, and with my left hand fixed upon his shoulder that I might not be separated from him, with my right I incessantly thrust back those whose aim seemed to be to tear him from limb to limb," he wrote Abby. "Scenes of excitement and peril are not new to me, but in all my past experience I have seen nothing like this. For a time it seemed impossible to save him from the fury of those whom he had so deeply injured, so grossly insulted. But fortune favored the courage and energy of his protectors, and to our great relief he was at length placed beyond the reach of danger. I have often been myself the object of popular rage, as you well know, but never did I feel half the anxiety for my own life which I felt for his, or make half the effort to save it. Here I felt that the honor of our cause was at stake, and for the moment I yearned for a bloodless victory."

Indeed, the victory was bloodless. The escort managed to get Butman to the train station, where he was locked into the privy for safekeeping. The train was not due for some time, and the slavecatcher was finally sent off in a hack, having given Stephen his solemn promise that he would never return to Worcester again.

Instead of thanking him for his part in the affair, however, the Worcester police brought charges against Stephen for creating a disturbance by watching Butman's hotel the night before.

At first Stephen refused to recognize the legal processes. Then he said he would stand trial if he could have Abby as his lawyer. The town was in an uproar at the thought. No woman had ever practiced law in Massachusetts; the mere thought was outlandish. On the other hand, was it illegal? Finally the court ruled that she could not appear since there was no precedent.

Stephen then undertook his own defense. Perhaps coached by Abby, he asked such penetrating questions of the witnesses that they became confused and their story unclear. Finally Stephen was acquitted. He was immensely pleased with himself.

"I am now fully satisfied that the only thing necessary to render the abolitionism of this city fully equal to any possible emergency is a competent leader; and the experience . . . has given me to believe that . . . I could fill that role," he wrote Abby jubilantly. For a time at least his confidence in himself as the most radical of the abolitionists was restored. Abby, who loved him, gloried in his triumph.

Later, when they thought back over the Butman affair, both Abby and Stephen were surprised to realize that it had been the nonresisters who were the most militant. Worcester was supposedly an abolitionist city, full of men and women who had no scruples about the use of force. Yet most of these had proved too timid to do anything when the hour came. "If blood ever flows in the streets of Worcester," Stephen remarked to a fellow pacifist, "it will be shed by non-resisters."

Abby complained in *The Liberator* that "if not even the city of Worcester was prepared to protect the slave with the force of arms then it is time to arouse such public sentiment as needed to give safety to the refugees."

The tension between their commitment to nonresistance, and their identification with the escaping slaves, continued to pull them this way and that, right up until the beginning of the Civil War.

# XVII

# *The Price of Devotion*

THE 1850s were a time of discouragement for abolitionists. More and more turned away from the old campaign and put their trust in political action.

Abby, however, refused to surrender, and insisted on trying harder, on giving more speeches, on raising more money, on circulating more antislavery papers. She drove herself unrelentingly, and as a result, paid a heavy price.

When he first heard her speak, William Lloyd Garrison's brother, James Garrison, said she had lungs like a boatswain. For years and years, in icy winter and in hot summer, in dusty halls and in huge outdoor amphitheaters, she had raised her voice until everyone present heard her perfectly.

Now, as she reached forty, Abby's golden voice began to go. Reporters for the first time complained that they couldn't hear her. At some conventions her remarks were recorded as "inaudible." More and more frequently she turned the meetings over to her traveling companion—whether Lucy

Stone, Susan Anthony, or Sallie Holley, daughter of Myron Holley, a founder of the Liberty party.

In the summer of 1851 Abby toured western New York State, raising money to support a trip to the United States by the famous British abolitionist, George Thompson. Word of her troubles with her voice reached Garrison, who promptly wrote to her, urging her to cut her speeches shorter by 50 percent. He heard that she sometimes spoke for two or three hours, he said. This was entirely too long not only for her voice but for her audiences. "Ordinarily a speech one hour long, however interesting, is long enough, and will produce the best effect," he advised.

Alarmed by the general state of Abby's health, as well as by her cracking voice, the Boston abolitionists soon found they had Stephen too to worry about. Stephen had left the farm in the fall of 1851 for a brief lecturing tour in Nantucket and Cape Cod. He returned ill, and soon developed chills and fever.

He tried his usual water-cure remedies, and Abby consulted a clairvoyant, but he grew progressively worse all fall. The abolitionists began to fear that he was dying of consumption. Early in December, Samuel May wrote letters to Abby and Stephen urging them to go to Jamaica for the winter. The American Anti-Slavery Society would pay their expenses, and they could earn the money by scouting out the islands as a settlement area for escaped slaves, he suggested.

Miraculously, Stephen recovered his health before the journey was to begin, and Abby decided to spend most of the winter with him in Worcester, making sure that he stayed healthy, and rested herself. By spring she was off again, however. The rest of 1852 she spent traveling back and forth across western New York State, raising money, gathering subscriptions for the *National Anti-Slavery Standard,* giving speeches whenever her voice was up to it.

In the fall of 1853 they were able to leave the farm together and travel in the West. It was like old times, with the press attacking them and audiences hostile. The Detroit *Daily Advertiser* referred to them as Mr. and Mrs. Kelley. Stephen was called "Mr. Abby," the henpecked husband whose wife wore the "trowsers." At a meeting in Plymouth, Michigan, a man charged that Abby had "taken up with a great buck nigger and after getting tired of him took up with Foster and by and by will get tired of Foster and take up with someone else." Fortunately Stephen was there to defend her.

"In the evening my husband called out the scamp and made him tremble," Abby reported.

Rumors, however, persisted: Abby and Stephen were not legally married; they believed in Fanny Wrightism, or no-marriage perfectionism. Crowds grew large and angry. In Detroit they were locked out of City Hall where they were scheduled to lecture. Stephen persuaded some local abolitionists to break the lock and help him take possession of the hall illegally. The meeting went off without violence, but William Lloyd Garrison, following behind the Fosters, highly disapproved of the procedure.

"Stephen and Abby, instead of facilitating my progress, appear to have given me an Irish hoist, 'a peg lower,' " he wrote home.

Abby herself wrote to Samuel May that Michigan brought back old memories:

> We are doing over again, in Michigan, what we did
> nearly fifteen years ago in New England, and eight

years ago in Ohio—fighting "New Organization"
here under the cover of Free Democracy. We little
dreamed, when we came here, what we should
encounter. It never occurred to us, that, as a matter of
course, this conflict must be passed [through]
everywhere before genuine anti-slavery could get a
substantial footing. When we went to Detroit, we
did not even know that the Free Soil paper was
edited by two priests. Indeed, we knew almost
nothing about it, though, since, we have learned that
it has always been thrusting a stab at Garrison when
it could find opportunity. But since Garrison and
ourselves were there, it has kept a constant stream
running from its vials of wrath, mainly on Garrison.

Together the Fosters lectured in the Midwest throughout
the winter. Stephen returned to the farm in April 1854 and
announced he wasn't going anywhere for a while, but Abby
continued to travel and lecture on and off for the rest of the
year. She was having more and more trouble with her throat,
and approaching exhaustion, but she was driven on by a
growing sense of urgency and despair.

Her letters to Alla in this period describe the hardships of
frontier life. She was eaten up with bedbugs, had to share a
chamber with a man and his wife, slept with the dirt from a
sod roof sifting down upon her. Her throat was almost
constantly inflamed.

It all finally caught up with her. By the summer of 1855
she was in a state of near-collapse. She looked so thin and sick
that her friends all begged her to take a year off for complete
rest.

Knowing that Abby worried constantly about money,

Wendell Phillips raised a substantial sum from the Boston abolitionists. It was enough to permit Abby to rest while receiving almost the same amount as she would get in salary as an agent.

In addition to this gift, Charles Hovey, a kindly philanthropist, wrote that since he was leaving a large sum in his will in the care of Abby and Stephen, he thought they ought to permit him to send them the interest from that time forward, even though he was still alive.

Abby accepted the help gratefully and sent Stephen in her place to visit Ohio and raise money for the *Bugle* in the fall. Stephen, as usual, didn't like the assignment. He complained of this wandering mode of life, and of his own health. After a visit with Benjamin and Lizzie Jones, he remarked that Lizzie would have made him a fine wife!

Despite this fussing, he was deeply worried about Abby. He wrote that he hoped she would regain the vigor he had so admired in her when he first met her. He said he knew a "Quaker doctor" who could cure her. When Abby asked how to get in touch with the Quaker doctor, Stephen said he belonged in the spirit world, and Abby would have to consult a medium.

Abby evidently felt well enough at one point to attempt some management of the farm, for Stephen objected:

> I am happy to learn that you are getting along so well at home, at least that you feel so well satisfied. But you cannot appreciate the importance of my presence there. That the men will be faithful I have no doubt, but that they will do all that needs to be done is by no means probable, unless I am there to direct. You are a capital housekeeper, and can make a

> very creditable anti-slavery speech, but I have but
> little confidence in your ability to manage a farm.
> However, I am glad you are having an opportunity
> to try your skill in that department also.

Despite the healthy farming life, Abby's recovery was slow. To her physical condition was added the depressing news from Kansas, where skirmishes between proslavery and Free State men finally broke out in civil war in May. The ardent abolitionist John Brown and four of his sons were accused of killing five proslavery settlers. The newly created antislavery Republican party seemed to her and to Stephen like their old enemies, the Liberty party or the Free Soil party, in new clothes. The farm was all mud and debts. It was a dreary time.

Finally, painfully, she began to get better. By 1857 she was well enough to assume the job of general agent of the Anti-Slavery Society. Thereafter she was busy raising money and organizing campaigns. She even spoke, when her voice would allow it. But she was no longer able to command audiences. She did best in small groups, where she was already known and people could strain to catch her words. Her days as a great orator were now behind her.

# XVIII

# "We Must Fire Up the Opposition"

IF Abby grew depressed by continued streams of bad news, she knew only one remedy. They must all simply work harder. Stephen, however, began to wonder if the old methods would work at all.

In February 1855 he had written a pamphlet, "Revolution the Only Remedy," which revealed the way his thoughts were trending. The old doctrine of disunion with church and state was not good enough any more, Stephen asserted. The abolitionists must support the slaves in bringing about a revolution of the whole system. He hoped it would be a peaceful revolution, but he was afraid it might be a bloody one. In the latter case, he implied, he would have to support it.

Among the Garrisonians, Stephen began to make himself more unpopular than ever. He criticized the American Anti-Slavery Society and its methods, said he was tired of "protestations," and questioned nonresistance. Violence was just as loving as nonviolence, he claimed at one point. After years of fighting first the Liberty party, then the Free Soilers, the abolitionists were now faced with the newly formed and broadly based Republican party, which was rapidly gathering all the antislavery forces to its banner. Stephen began to wonder once more whether the Garrisonian stand against voting was ever going to work.

"There are few here who do not desire a dissolution of the Union," he wrote Abby in the fall of 1855, when on a lecture tour in Ohio. "But vote they must, vote they will, come what may; and so long as there is no way provided for them to vote in harmony with our principles, they will continue to be thrown into an antagonistic position."

The breach between Stephen and the Garrisonians grew wider at the American Anti-Slavery Society's annual meeting in May 1856. Just prior to the meeting, Massachusetts antislavery Senator Charles Sumner had been viciously beaten about the head with a heavy cane by a hotheaded young Southerner, Preston Brooks, in retaliation for some remarks of Sumner's in a famous speech, "The Crime Against Kansas." Garrison and his colleagues had often differed with Sumner, but under the circumstances they decided to pass a resolution praising his bravery.

Foster, however, would not join in. "Who is Charles Sumner," Stephen asked rhetorically, "that this Society should espouse his quarrels with the slaveholders?" Any man who sat in the U.S. Senate was part of a system that upheld slavery, in Stephen's view. If he did not want to be part of it, he ought to pack up and come home.

As much a purist as her husband, Abby also refused to support the resolution praising Sumner. In an eloquent speech, which brought her at least one letter from a grateful admirer, she expressed her support for her husband. She was going to be loyal to both Stephen and the Anti-Slavery Society, come what may.

The final break between Stephen and the Garrisonians came the following winter. Samuel May, then the general agent of the Anti-Slavery Society, persuaded Stephen to make a lecture tour through the southern counties of western New York State. Susan B. Anthony was to go ahead of him and set up the meetings. Lizzie and Benjamin Jones, of Ohio, were to accompany him.

Stephen set out with good spirit, but everything seemed to go wrong. The weather was bad and the snow deep, preventing him from keeping some appointments. Susan's arrangements were careless. Sometimes he would arrive in a town and find that no advance preparations had been made at all.

After a few weeks of this, Stephen decided he was needed in Worcester. He dropped the lecture series in midstream, went home, and wrote Samuel May an angry letter, accusing him of sitting snugly in his study and ordering other people to do the hard work of antislavery lecturing.

Angry, May wrote back that perhaps Stephen ought not to be employed as an antislavery lecturer anymore. Later he retracted the statement, but Stephen was a proud man. From that time onward he never accepted a salary from the society, scarcely considered himself a member, and lectured only as a volunteer.

Shortly after the fracas with Stephen, May resigned, and Abby became the general agent. It meant that she was becoming more closely tied than ever to the old society, just as Stephen was breaking from it.

The differences between the Fosters came into the open at the antislavery meeting the next year. In response to Abby's heartfelt appeal for redoubled efforts, Stephen said, "It cannot be done . . . the old agencies are no longer sufficient."

Torn between her loyalties to her husband and to the society, Abby did what she could to make peace. After she became general agent she sat in on the meetings of the executive committee. From this vantage point she wrote Stephen that the other members were much closer to his way of thinking than he realized. Against his wishes she considered raising the question of his being made agent again before the committee. She determined to do so only if she could produce a unanimous vote in his favor. Unfortunately, some members were opposed.

As general agent, Abby was the society's chief fundraiser. Maria Chapman tutored her ("She knows what cord to touch in every heart," Abby reported), and she went to call on wealthy Bostonians such as James Russell Lowell and Longfellow. Sometimes in this fashion she raised as much as five hundred dollars in a single afternoon. It was a lot different from the early days in Ohio when she went from door to door, collecting twenty-five cents at a time. Still, she often failed to find people at home, and she was dreadfully tired by night.

More to her liking were appeals at mass meetings. At one such meeting she pledged herself to mortgage her own farm if necessary to keep money in the antislavery coffers.

"I feel that to leave my daughter a home, to leave her even a dollar in money, when by sacrificing that home, or by expending that money I could leave her freedom would be violating a trust that God has committed to my care," she announced solemnly.

Whenever she went to Boston, William Lloyd Garrison and his wife, Helen, insisted that Abby stay with them. This Abby didn't much care to do. There was a growing coolness between her husband and Garrison that put her in an awkward position. Worse, she was becoming convinced that the real trouble in the Anti-Slavery Society was being caused by Garrison himself.

For Garrison, too, was changing. Like Stephen, he was beginning to lose faith in the old methods. Unlike Stephen, he saw hope in the new Republican party. When John Frémont ran as a Republican in 1856, Garrison said in *The Liberator*, "If there were no moral barrier to our voting and we had a million votes to bestow, we should cast them all for Frémont."

Garrison still believed that voting itself wrongly acknowledged the Constitution and government that was making slavery possible, but his thinking was becoming more tortured.

All this made Abby uncomfortable accepting the Garrisons' hospitality. Still she was determined to "bear much for the cause sake. . . . What if Garrison shall snap me up as if I were a puppy, he turns around to strike off the head of the frothing mad dog that is pouncing on slaves and I will help him in my small way," she wrote.

In the spring of 1857, the Supreme Court reviewed the case of Dred Scott, a slave who claimed his freedom on the basis of having lived in a free state and a free territory for several years. The Court ruled against him, claiming he was not a citizen of the United States and ruling that the Missouri Compromise was unconstitutional because it deprived slave-owners of their property without due process of law.

The abolitionists were further disheartened and driven to extremes by this ruling. Stephen began talking about organizing an antislavery party. Abby decided, despite her failing voice and strength, to make a lecture tour of her beloved Ohio in the fall.

Writing in the *Standard* from Middlebury, Ohio, in September, she said she found the abolitionists there disillusioned after two years of Republican administration in that state, and ready to hear the true word.

"The proposition is as clear to me as any in mathematics, that could the means be put into our hands, before another Presidential campaign shall occur, we should fill the entire North with such a flood of light that the system of darkness would skulk forever from the North, and then, of necessity, speedily perish," she wrote to the editor of the *National Anti-Slavery Standard*. Undoubtedly she hoped that Garrison would read and heed what she said.

The Western campaign, planned and executed by Abby, was to culminate in a Disunion Convention in Cleveland. Abby left for the West, confident that all the most important abolitionists would join her in Ohio for this major event. There was a financial panic in the fall of 1857, however, and because of it, Garrison attempted to cancel the convention. Abby, Stephen, and perhaps twenty other abolitionists met anyway and criticized the fainthearted.

"The great pecuniary distress that afflicts the country is mentioned as a reason why the Northern Convention should be put off," Abby said. "I believe this is a reason why it should not be put off."

Cut down to a handful of the most radical abolitionists, the convention was fiery indeed. In various speeches the slaves were exhorted to arise in bloody rebellion and the individual states to secede from the Union. The Union itself was described as "a crime and a curse that should not exist a single hour."

It was at this convention that Abby made the most radical speech of her career. "Ours is a revolution, not a reform," she said. "We contemplate the entire destruction of the present National Government and Union. . . . We must fire up the opposition, and create such a spirit of resistance that our opponents will be pushed to extremes. The Republican party must be driven over to the enemy, as it will not take the true position. The battle must be fought face to face."

From Cleveland the Fosters went home to Worcester, looking forward to spending the Christmas holidays with their beloved Alla. The girl was ten—tall, thin, and inclined to stoop. They had worried about her posture before; over the holidays they decided the problem was serious enough to take her to a Boston doctor.

The medical report they received was not encouraging. Alla had a spinal ailment of serious nature. She must wear a brace and lie flat as much as possible.

Distraught with worry, Abby spent most of the next year at Alla's bedside, traveling only enough to keep up her duties as general agent for the Anti-Slavery Society. Friends of the Fosters wrote from all over to inquire about the little girl's health, to offer help and sympathy. Many were glad to note that because of Alla's situation Abby herself was getting more needed rest.

Alla was lonely for the companionship of other children her age. Perhaps partly for this reason, Abby invited the two youngest Garrison children to spend the summer on the farm.

Fanny and Frank returned to their parents in the fall with rosy cheeks and good appetites. Garrison wrote a cordial letter to Stephen and Abby, thanking them for their hospitality. It seemed for a while as though the breach was going to mend.

It didn't, however. The Fosters couldn't forgive Garrison his continued drift toward the Republican party. In January 1859, at the Massachusetts Anti-Slavery Convention, Abby complained that it was hard to rebuke the Republicans because "they are so near to us." "Nevertheless rebuke is needed," she continued, "because our work is to be done all over again."

Garrison was angry, and made some personal remarks about Abby's cracked voice and graying hair. These she decided to ignore. An uneasy peace prevailed until the New England convention in May. Here Stephen created trouble by implying that any abolitionist who supported the Republicans lacked integrity.

Furious, Garrison lashed back by attacking not Stephen but Abby, even though Abby wasn't present in the hall. Abby went around collecting funds for the Anti-Slavery Society from the Republicans, he charged, and in order to please them, pretended to agree with their views. Then she attacked them behind their backs. Who lacked integrity under these circumstances?

The hall sat in stunned silence as Garrison left the podium. Both Stephen and Parker Pillsbury met him in the wings and demanded that he instantly retract his insulting remarks, but this he refused to do.

Abby was staying with the Garrisons at the time and was already in bed for the night when the fatal speech was made. Very early the next morning Stephen came by to tell her what had been said. She thereupon got dressed and flew out of the house before breakfast in order to avoid seeing Garrison again. A relationship of thirty years' standing was shattered.

Abby had been hurt before, and hurt often by aspersions about her supposed sexual laxity. For years the cry of "Jezebel" had echoed in her ears. Only the past summer a minister in New Hampshire had dared to say something to Stephen about "that woman who pretends to be your wife." All this had pained Abby deeply, and brought tears to her eyes. Nevertheless, thinking it was right to accept such abuse for the sake of the slave, she had gone right on with her activities.

Now, however, William Lloyd Garrison had questioned her honesty. How could she continue to collect money for the Anti-Slavery Society under such a cloud? With her voice gone, what could she do but raise funds? Garrison seemed to have destroyed completely her usefulness to the cause to which she had given her life. Heartbroken, she went back home to Worcester.

Garrison wrote her a long letter of explanation, but not apology. He had said nothing wrong. If she had a complaint against him, she should have raised it with him, rather than leaving his house like that. He had certainly not meant to impeach her personal integrity. "I have always regarded you as peerless—the moral Joan of Arc of the World." No, he simply wanted to make clear the "inconsistency and practical wrongfulness" of her course.

Abby was not appeased. Only a public apology, she wrote Garrison, would erase from the public mind the idea that she was dishonest. Only after such an apology would she be able to solicit funds again.

The two exchanged another set of long letters, but Garrison continued to justify himself, claiming that he was not a "wrong doer," and implying that in her state of mind Abby was not capable of serving as financial agent of the Anti-Slavery Society.

Abby finally gave up. Across the last letter from Garrison she wrote, "No. 3 which has never been answered because I cannot afford to again defend myself against the charge of falsehood."

The split with Garrison meant for Abby a gradual withdrawal from her many activities with the Anti-Slavery Society. Her first action was to submit her resignation to the Massachusetts board. Wendell Phillips, who was trying desperately to hold the organization together, pleaded with her to remain. Was not the board big enough to allow for differences of opinion?

Abby, however, was adamant. "I have escaped from the priestly rule of the church, from the demagoguism of politicians, from the tyrany [sic] of society. Heaven save me from any other dictatorship though it come in the mantle of the slave's best friend."

Abby's radicalism had pushed her to the fringes of the women's rights movement eight years earlier. Now she was to become an outsider to the Anti-Slavery Society, to which she had given over half her life. She and Stephen had together "fired up the opposition and pushed it to extremes."

# XIX

# *Mine Eyes Have Seen the Glory*

IN October the news came: John Brown and eighteen men had seized the federal arsenal at Harpers Ferry and held some local citizens captive. It was to have been the first step in an insurrection of the slaves, but none came to his relief, and several days later he was taken and charged with treason.

Stephen reacted to Brown's act with mixed feelings. Ever since Nat Turner had led a slave rebellion in Virginia in 1831, Stephen had been longing for such an uprising. On the other hand, despite his earlier wavering, he was still committed to nonresistance. The revolution of economic, political, and social institutions for which he yearned was too sweeping to be accomplished by force of arms.

Abby, of course, had never wavered in her pacifism. In sorrow and dismay, the Fosters watched as many of their former colleagues forgot their scruples and threw themselves into partisan support for Brown. Theodore Parker, Thomas Higginson, and Gerrit Smith had been among those who actually financed the insurrection. Ralph Waldo Emerson,

Henry David Thoreau, and Lydia Maria Child wrote, singing his praises. Even Garrison inched further away from nonresistance. What was becoming of the old crusade?

Stephen buried his frustration by deciding to study the Constitution of the United States more closely in light of the raids. He had been calling it an agreement with death and a covenant with hell all these years. Now, looking at it in a fresh light, he was able to see it as a potentially antislavery document. The fact that it did not refer specifically to slavery at all suggested that it did not recognize it. Rather it was bound by the Bill of Rights to guarantee justice to all citizens.

It is hard to know whether Stephen really saw the Constitution differently or just wanted to find justification for at last yielding to his longstanding temptation to be active in politics. At the Massachusetts Anti-Slavery Society meeting in January 1860, he told about his new interpretation and announced that on the basis of it he was going to organize an antislavery party.

The Republicans were campaigning against the spread of slavery to any more states or territories, but there was no word in their platform about emancipation. Stephen's new party would proclaim the end of slavery in all the states, based on constitutional law and enforced by the federal government.

As might be expected, most members of the Anti-Slavery Society were cool to Stephen's proposal. They were still committed to disunion, though some were wavering toward support of the Republicans. Stephen's platform was remarkably like that of the Radical Abolitionists, the group which had once supported the Liberty party, later supported the Free Soil party, and now was running Gerrit Smith for President. After years of fighting the voting abolitionists, the Garrisonians were not ready to switch.

Nevertheless, Stephen spent the spring and summer organizing his new party, and in September actually held a convention in Worcester. The local paper estimated attendance at thirty to eighty by day, two to three hundred by night. Of the few prominent abolitionists who did attend, only Frederick Douglass supported Stephen. The convention formed a new party, the Union Democratic party, but failed to nominate any candidates.

Abby remained true to her nonresistance, disunion principles and did not support Stephen in his short-lived career as a politician. Instead she went off alone to Ohio to try once more to lure her old converts from the arms of the Republicans. She was suffering from stomach trouble, her voice was cracked, and she dreaded being away from Alla, who was still not well. Nevertheless, she once more followed the rugged path of duty.

The Republican candidate, Abraham Lincoln, was a puzzle to many abolitionists. He had announced himself to be personally opposed to slavery, but he did not believe in emancipation, nor in racial integration. He was opposed to the spread of slavery but equally opposed to immediate emancipation in the District of Columbia or the repeal of the Fugitive Slave Law. He said that "this government cannot endure permanently, half slave and half free" but he also said he had no idea how to get rid of the institution of slavery.

Abby, however, was not puzzled. As uncompromising as ever, she was sure that whoever was not with her was against her. At the annual antislavery celebration on July 4 at

Framingham, Massachusetts, she attacked the Republicans vigorously.

A month later, at a spiritualist convention in Rhode Island, she said that no effort to elevate women through women's rights or spiritualism could do any good while two million black women were forced into prostitution and blamed Democrats and Republicans equally for the maintenance of slavery.

Now, back in Ohio, she went from town to town, visiting places that had changed markedly in the fifteen years since her first campaigns, looking up old converts, trying desperately to warn them against "the Slave Hound of Illinois," as she and others sometimes called Lincoln.

She was still out West in chilly November when the election was held. Lincoln won, carrying 18 free states and 180 electoral votes. Even her old friend Wendell Phillips hailed the election as a great step forward. "For the first time in our history the slave has chosen a President of the United States. We have passed a Rubicon . . . ," he said. But Abby was only downhearted. The people had been deceived.

A month after the election, South Carolina seceded from the Union, followed in quick succession by ten other states. After some initial misgivings, most of the Garrisonians decided this was to the good. Without the support of federal troops, the Southerners would never be able to keep down the slave revolts which were bound to occur. Other slaves would run away, and the Northerners would no longer be forced to return them. The South would be isolated from the rest of the United States and held up to the criticism of the world.

Stephen and Abby, however, thought this was deserting the

slave. "I do not see how the slaves could possibly be benefited by a political separation from the North, where most of their active friends now reside," Stephen said. When they preached disunion, this was not the disunion they had meant.

With a brief visit home, Abby spent most of "secession winter" in Ohio. Still wearily working away in April 1861, she predicted in a speech at Cleveland that the Union between the South and the North could not hold together. She would not be surprised, she said, if war would break out in six days. (In fact, it did.) She would "shed no tears over it for it would be war between the North and the South, and when rogues fall out, honest men get their dues."

On April 12 the rebels opened fire on Fort Sumter, and the Civil War began. A wave of patriotism swept the North, and the abolitionists, who had been despised and mobbed just a few months before, became heroes and heroines. The President himself spoke for the masses in saying he was fighting to preserve the Union, not to abolish slavery. Still, the abolitionists could not help believing that freedom for the slaves would be the result.

William Lloyd Garrison now announced that despite his peace principles he was wholeheartedly behind the war. Most of his followers echoed his sentiments. Late in 1861 he changed the old superscription on *The Liberator* from "The United States Constitution is a covenant with death and an agreement with hell" to a new model: "Proclaim liberty throughout the land, to all the inhabitants thereof."

Many people, of course, called his inconsistency to his attention. Some he answered defensively, but to others he responded lightly, paraphrasing Shakespeare, "When I said I would not sustain the Constitution because it was a 'covenant with death, and an agreement with hell,' I had no idea I would live to see death and hell secede."

To the Fosters, Garrison's desertion of the old doctrines was no laughing matter. At the Framingham meeting in July, they raised strenuous objections to the spectacle of nonresistant abolitionists in full support of government, and tried to get their old comrades to demand immediate emancipation. The Garrisonians, however, were now wholeheartedly behind the Civil War. The Fosters' resolution was laid upon the table.

Some of the enthusiasm of the abolitionists for the Lincoln Administration began to cool the following year when the President seemed unwilling to make any move to free the slaves, even in the District of Columbia. Lincoln appeared determined to uphold slavery, permitting army officers to return refugees to their masters, and making no move to end the slave trade or the extension of slavery into the territories. When he did begin to talk about freeing the slaves of the District, it was to be accomplished by paying their masters. This was "compensation," a practice which the abolitionists had formally abhorred.

The whole sorry mess was not really Lincoln's fault, Stephen argued in early 1862. It was the people, who were the rulers of the land, who ought to force him to what was right. The abolition societies had been formed to change the hearts and minds of the people, and they must continue. He was back once more in agreement with Abby on the need for the old methods.

At the annual meeting of the Anti-Slavery Society, held as usual that May, Abby noted the tendency of abolitionists to compromise. "We seem to be partaking in the general corruption of the times," she noted. "Age tends to conservatism, and we should pray to be preserved in the freshness of our fanaticism."

Unless the abolitionists continued the great work they had undertaken of getting rid of prejudice, she feared that "the hate of the colored race will continue and the poison of this wickedness will destroy us as a nation."

When emancipation was finally proclaimed in January of 1863, Stephen, Abby, and a few of their radical friends were unhappy with its provisions. It was limited to states actually in rebellion against the Union, thus leaving slavery perfectly legal in the border states. The proclamation also announced that the real object of the war was preservation of the Union, not the end of slavery, and suggested that slaveholders should be compensated when possible.

"How cold the President's proclamation is—graceless, coming from a sinner at the head of a nation of sinners—of course such pride must be humbled before God," Sallie Holley wrote to them, exactly echoing their own sentiments.

Led by William Lloyd Garrison, most of the executive committee of the American Anti-Slavery Society, however, were overjoyed by the proclamation. They felt that their work was now done, and threw all their time and money into a support of the war effort. The old societies were allowed to continue, but they were now mere forms.

All this pained Abby. Now, she believed, was the time to be out lecturing, raising money, selling subscriptions, preaching the gospel of true equality. Emancipation would only work if it grew out of a nationwide conviction that slavery and color prejudice were wrong. Any gains for the slave won on the battlefield would otherwise be quickly lost upon reunion.

Holding these views, Abby could not take part in the societies organized to aid the freedmen. What was needed, she said, was justice, not charity. Nor could she join the Loyal Women of the Republic, organized by Elizabeth Cady Stanton and Susan B. Anthony in the spring of 1863. The government ought to be scolded, she argued, not supported by its old critics.

As the war dragged on, Abby's opposition to it made her more and more isolated. She stayed home in Worcester most of the time, venturing forth only to attend the antislavery meetings. What was the use of traveling about in a land where people seemed to have lost their reason? Besides, she was ill and Alla still sickly.

Even her correspondence dwindled to almost nothing at this time. Stephen was with her, so there was no need for these two to exchange long letters. Sydney Gay was now managing editor of the New York *Tribune* and a war supporter. Maria Chapman no longer wrote. Only Sallie Holley, Abby's old traveling companion, kept up a steady stream of letters.

It was a welcome respite from all the dreariness when Abby found one project in which she could join her old comrades. The Loyal Women of the Republic decided to make its major project the gathering of one million signatures on a petition to support the Thirteenth Amendment, forever abolishing slavery in the United States. This was indeed the sort of business abolitionists should be about, Abby thought.

Since she and Stephen now sat on the board of the Charles Hovey Foundation, they were able to help Susan B. Anthony obtain money for the campaign from that source. Better yet,

Abby could circulate the petition in Worcester. Never happier than when she had a practical job to do, Abby went at it with a will. It was like old times in Lynn.

The women did not manage to collect 1,000,000 signatures, but they gathered an impressive 400,000. The Thirteenth Amendment was finally ratified in January 1865, much to Abby's delight.

In the months preceding ratification, Abby and Stephen had found little to be happy about. Not only had the Lincoln Administration delayed emancipation: Lincoln himself had several times overridden his generals when they declared all slaves to be free in captured territories. White officers were put in charge of black troops, and black soldiers given less pay for equal risks. White Southern officers were coddled when captured, while the escaped blacks, called contraband of war, were treated harshly.

Worse yet, as Northern armies advanced into the South and the generals began to put reconstruction plans to work in captured areas, it became clear that no radical change was contemplated. Stephen and Abby, like most abolitionists, believed that large rebel holdings should be confiscated, and each freed slave given some land to farm, but this was done only rarely and timidly.

To support such a régime seemed to Abby like desertion of the high ground of principle upon which she had based her life. Yet Garrison was becoming more enthusiastic about Lincoln with each passing day. It was a disgrace to the American Anti-Slavery Society.

As time passed, the influential Wendell Phillips came to support the Fosters' point of view, and a new radical wing formed within the society. A new schism was begun.

At the January 1864 meeting of the Massachusetts Anti-Slavery Society, the radicals were able to win a majority on the business committee. Among those elected were Abby and Stephen. At the May meeting Stephen made a stirring speech, asking how the abolitionists could consider endorsing Lincoln for a second term when he had returned more fugitive slaves than any previous President. Wendell Phillips proposed two resolutions favoring a more egalitarian form of reconstruction. Again, the radicals won the day.

In the course of the summer, Garrison came out for Lincoln, while Phillips supported the more radical Frémont. The American Anti-Slavery Society was now clearly split into two factions.

The rift created tension between Abby and her old friend and mentor Maria Chapman. Maria had supported Abby until the war broke out. Then she threw herself into the work of the freedmen's associations and the support of the war effort. Neither she nor her sister, Anna Weston, would give one penny for the campaign to support the constitutional amendment against slavery.

Abby took their defection bitterly. At the next January meeting of the Massachusetts Anti-Slavery Society she moved that the two be excused from duty on the board, "since they believed the work of the Society already done."

Even the end of the war, in April 1865, and the tragic assassination of President Lincoln a few days later, did not cool down the battle within the Anti-Slavery Society. The anniversary meeting held in New York in May was the scene of struggle. This time the black abolitionists—Charles Remond, Frederick Douglass, and Robert Purvis—joined their white radical comrades in arguing that the Garrisonians were deserting the black man. Someone quoted Andrew Johnson, President since Lincoln's assassination, as having said that he was "willing to send every Negro in the country to Africa to save the Union and sink the whole black race 10 thousand fathoms deep to effect the same object." It seemed suddenly clear that emancipation was not enough.

By a vote of 118 to 40, the radicals won control of the society and defeated a measure to dissolve it. Later the same month, a similar victory was achieved at the New England Anti-Slavery Society meeting.

After the vote, Abby got to her feet. The new society under new leadership would need support badly, she said. In fact, it would need funds. Who was there in the hall who would not pledge a dollar to such a cause?

It was one of hundreds and hundreds of such speeches Abby had made for the American Anti-Slavery Society. But sadly, in this hour of victory, her poor voice was inaudible.

# XX

# *"Am I Not a Woman and a Sister?"*

EVERY day the news from the South got worse. Blacks were being moved off the land they had been given to farm, barred from juries, sold into temporary bondage for vagrancy. Erstwhile rebels were free to lynch and whip their former slaves. Rape was common.

Abby and Stephen knew only one sure remedy for this: Give the vote to the black, along with land ownership. "There is no safety for man's liberty in this country until he is armed with the shield of suffrage," Stephen declared.

At first the radical abolitionists hoped that suffrage for the blacks could be made a condition of readmission of the rebel states to the Union. But this hope faded as Andrew Johnson proved himself to be prejudiced against the blacks and opposed to any sort of transformation of the society of the South.

Congress passed the Fourteenth Amendment, making all persons—including blacks—citizens, and guaranteeing federal protection of their equal rights. Southern states were allowed to rejoin the Union once they ratified this amendment.

Most abolitionists opposed this as a half measure. "The Negro will never be thoroughly protected, even in person and property, until he has the ballot," Theodore Tilton, the editor of the *Independent,* said.

After the congressional elections of 1866, when Johnson deserted the Republicans and tried to form a new conservative party, the abolitionists were united in working for his impeachment. He was tried, but by the margin of one vote found not guilty by the Senate in 1867. At the same time the abolitionists mounted a fresh and vigorous campaign for black suffrage.

But now a difference of opinion arose between the Fosters. If the abolitionists were going to press for the black's right to vote, why not the woman's as well? Stephen thought the two causes could be combined. Abby felt that conditions in the South demanded that the blacks have priority.

At an antislavery meeting early in 1866 they tangled in public. When Lucy Stone spoke, asking the members of the American Anti-Slavery Society to support a fight to make the suffrage issue regardless of sex, Abby rebuked her.

"The attention of this Society should be concentrated solely on the claims of the colored race," she said tartly.

"In season and out the claims of woman to her political rights should be urged, but I am glad to maintain the rights of the Negro also," Lucy said.

Stephen said he saw no reason not to connect the two.

For months the disagreement simmered. Early in 1867, Lucy wrote Abby a long, emotional letter, reproaching her for her stand. "I sit down to write you with a feeling of despair which never came to me before where a principle is involved," she wrote. ". . . You, and Phillips and Garrison, and the brave workers, who for thirty years have said 'let justice be done, if the heavens fall,' now smitten by a strange blindness, believe that the Nation's peril can be averted, if it can be induced to accept the poor half-loaf of justice for the Negro, poisoned by its lack of justice for every woman in the land. As if the application of a universal principle to a single class could suffice for the necessity of this hour! . . . O Abby, it is a terrible mistake you are all making."

Abby brooded over the letter for two weeks, then wrote back to say she felt sure Lucy was overwrought or she would never have said such things. "We have already got more for the Negro than I expected to live to see, and a great deal better prospects for woman than my most sanguine hopes ever pictured me, tho the struggle for the equality of woman was with me, antecedent to the struggle for the slave," she wrote.

"Indeed, I doubt whether I should ever have had the strength to carry me before the public for the slave had I not seen that in so doing I was practically doing even more for woman. None of the women who preceded me on the antislavery platform took that position as a matter of right, but of sufferance. . . . I pleaded with those who I felt could do the work for a whole year, and finding they would not do it, I took my position, that is, I blew my ram's horn and so the war was opened. And yet it [the woman question] has ever been heretofore as now, incidental, and this is and ever has been my reason for thus making it. The slave is more deeply wronged than woman, and why any nation can be so infernal as to keep him a chattel, it cannot be induced to allow political rights to a woman."

The woman question was broader, more important, more comprehensive, she went on, but the blacks' need was more pressing. It was just a matter of priorities. If Lucy saw a different path to follow, she wished her well, just as she had wished her well nearly twenty years ago. Meanwhile, Lucy must avoid overdoing, or she might find herself as ill as Abby now was.

Indeed, Abby was in serious shape. She had developed an ovarian cyst and needed an operation. In those days, surgery for this sort of condition was in its infancy, and no one quite knew how to treat the ailment. After exhausting the competence of local doctors, Abby came to New York in the spring of 1867 to see a specialist. While in the city, she could not resist attending a meeting of the newly formed American Equal Rights Association. She had not planned to speak, but an argument advanced by her old friend Elizabeth Cady Stanton brought her to her feet.

Stanton argued that it was dangerous both to the nation as a whole and to women to give the vote to uneducated black males while denying it to educated white women. "If all men are to vote, black and white, lettered and unlettered, washed and unwashed, the safety of the nation as well as the interest of women demand that we outweigh this incoming tide of ignorance, poverty, and vice, with the virtue, wealth, and education of the women of the country."

Sick, and scarcely able to make herself audible, Abby rose to insist once more that the blacks' need was greater than that of women. "He is treated as a slave today in several districts of the South. Without wages, without family rights, whipped and beaten by thousands, given up to the most horrible outrages, without the protection that his value as property formerly gave him. Have we no true sense of justice, are we not dead to the sentiments of humanity if we shall wish to postpone his security against present woes and future enslavement till woman shall obtain her political rights?"

Among those apparently not impressed by her argument was Stephen. He continued to believe that both as a matter of principle and of strategy the antislavery societies should struggle for suffrage without regard to color or sex. At the American Anti-Slavery Society's May meeting a few days later, he introduced a resolution to that effect. When the president ruled it out of order he appealed, pointing out that "the question of sex had early come up in this Society, and the Society had recognized the right of women to speak upon its platform in behalf of the slave."

All eyes turned to Abby. It was her right to speak to which Stephen referred. Abby, however, was not to be lured into the trap. It was not a question of sex, she replied. Women had demanded the right to speak, and the society had said it had no right to refuse to allow them to speak.

There followed a lively public exchange between husband and wife. Stephen pointed to the employment of women as agents of the society, again looking at Abby. Abby said that the society had claimed the right to employ whom it pleased; the liberty to know no sex, but souls.

Stephen tried to compromise: "If the ballot is demanded for the Negro, why not demand it for every Negro, male and female alike?" Abby was implacable.

Again, two weeks later, at the New England meeting, the two tangled. Stephen once more tried to argue that the question of suffrage for women ought to be pushed by the abolition societies. Wendell Phillips disagreed, and Abby backed him up against her husband.

"There is an Equal Rights Association of which I am a member," she said. "When I go there, I go there to secure suffrage for the man and woman without distinction of race, color, or condition. I go there as a suffrage woman, for the one purpose of securing suffrage for all; but when I come here, I come here to secure freedom from chattel slavery." The antislavery societies were not concerned with suffrage as an end itself but only as a means to provide the blacks with their freedom, she argued.

Thereafter the two agreed to disagree for a while. Stephen continued to argue for joining the issues. Abby instead gave what little time and strength she had to working for the vote for all black men.

In July of 1868 Abby was finally operated on for her cyst. So well-known was she, and so unusual the operation, that it was reported in the *National Anti-Slavery Standard.* The doctor said she had been very brave and had come out of her anesthesia in a blissful state, thanking God for her deliverance.

She was told to rest completely after the operation but was soon back at work, lobbying for black suffrage. When she attended the New England Women's Rights Convention that fall, it was to plead for the black.

"Many in that Convention who did not care a straw for him [the black]—who hardly knew him, had their memories jogged, and I doubt not, in many cases, their sympathies, for the first time awakened for him," she wrote in a letter to the editor of the *Standard.*

Stephen meanwhile decided to devote himself to educating the public to the woman issue. In Worcester he organized a series of weekly discussion meetings on this question. At one such gathering he challenged the idea that women who went out into public life were poor housekeepers. He would like, he said, to compare such women with those of the opposition.

"He paid high tribute to the character and faithfulness of his own mother and wife in this respect," a newspaper account reported. "And he demanded that the assertion that an interest in public affairs would detract from a woman's usefulness in the home circle should be supported by evidence, or abandoned."

In January 1869 Stephen tried once more to get the Massachusetts Anti-Slavery Society to go on record as supporting both black and woman's suffrage, but again met with rebuff. In February, when the Fifteenth Amendment was proposed by Congress referring to "race, color, and previous condition of servitude," but not sex, he gave up the battle and decided to support it.

Some members of the Equal Rights Association, however, decided otherwise. In *Revolution,* a feminist publication, a wealthy male supporter of the feminist movement wrote an article entitled "That Infamous Fifteenth Amendment," arguing once more that what was wanted was educated suffrage, and that educated women ought to be getting the ballot before the poor, ignorant blacks.

Radicals like the Fosters were opposed to the concept of education as the basis for the vote for anyone. It was a right, not something to be earned. The ignorance of the blacks in the South was due to slavery. They should not be penalized for the wicked system that was responsible for their condition.

Stephen was therefore angered by this article. At the May meeting of the Equal Rights Association, he demanded that Elizabeth Cady Stanton resign as president because of her connection with *Revolution.*

"It is true it [the article] was not written by our President, yet it comes from a person whom she has over and over publicly endorsed," Stephen said. "I am not willing to take George Francis Train [the author] on this platform with his ridicule of the Negro and opposition to his enfranchisement."

And with a few parting blasts he resigned.

Abby was sure in her own mind that once the blacks received the vote, women would follow in a year or so. As soon as the Fifteenth Amendment was ratified, she threw herself wholeheartedly into the women's rights movement. She was by now, however, too old, and too ill, and had made herself too unpopular, to achieve the leadership she had richly earned.

# XXI

# *The Many Fields of Reform*

THE ratification of the Fifteenth Amendment in March 1870 was a turning point in the life of Abby Kelley Foster. Up to that moment all her adult years had been concentrated on working through the American Anti-Slavery Society for the end of slavery. Now it seemed to many that that end had been accomplished.

True, there had been no radical redistribution of land in the South. Stephen continually warned that if justice weren't done for the ex-slaves, they would rise in defense of their own rights. He sometimes offered to rise with them, though he said he would lead his armies with the weapons of nonresistance.

"God made the earth, not for the rich man, not for the man who had a rich father, but for you and for me; as much for me, the son of a pauper, as you, the son of a millionaire, and I can recognize no law which secures you a farm, and makes me dependent on you for a place to lay my head at night," he once declared.

The rest of the abolitionists, however, believed that land reform would follow in due course once the blacks had the vote. In April 1870, the American Anti-Slavery Society was dissolved. Though they promptly helped to organize the Reform League to continue some aspects of the struggle, Abby and Stephen found the moment painful. Their beloved cause was still with them, but the institution into which they had channeled their energies for almost thirty-five years was no more.

But Abby was a person who never wasted time "in useless repining over the inevitable," according to her daughter, Alla, and Stephen was equally philosophic. Together they devoted the next years to a whole series of reform movements.

Abby had once written to Stephen that when slavery was ended there would remain "thick clouds and deep blackness to remove." Now it was time to get after the blackness.

Their primary concern was women's rights. In January 1870 they both spoke at the first meeting of the Massachusetts Woman Suffrage Association, and remained thereafter devoted members.

Another issue was temperance. Abby and Stephen had always been opposed to the use of alcohol. Now they had time to campaign against the grogshops which in their view blighted Worcester, now grown to an industrial city.

Stephen found out which church members sold liquor and denounced them with his old fire. Abby campaigned against licensing grogshops at all, and distributed no-license ballots at the polls. The voter who accepted one of her ballots would pledge himself to endorse no candidate who supported licensing.

Stephen also was interested in labor reform, although he

was opposed to the infant labor unions as narrow and clannish. He wanted instead to organize a national labor party, but never got beyond the idea stage.

Both Fosters kept up their enmity to the church. Reform was religion to Abby and Stephen, and there was no other. Did not Jesus Christ go around doing good? Did he not bid his followers to do likewise?

Abby had once written her sister and brother-in-law that "endeavors to improve mankind is the only object worth living for." Now, in 1870, Stephen expressed the same sentiment for both of them in a letter to George Thompson:

> The woman suffrage movement, for the last year and a half has sat heavily on my shoulders. The labor question, just struggling into existence but still enveloped in midnight darkness, demands both sympathy and work while the appalling evils of drunkenness which already threaten the overthrow of the republic call loudly for fresh consecration to that temperance cause.
>
> When I look around upon the *mountains of work* which rise before me in so many fields of reform, and the scattered few who are willing to do anything for the public weal disconnected with their own selfish ends, my hope of leisure vanishes into the darkness of despair, and I feel that for me, at least, there will be no rest till I find it in the upper world.

One way to work for women's rights was to make sure that their own daughter, Alla, had the best possible education. In the fall of 1868 she entered Vassar College.

"What she will do in life, time alone can tell, but in the absence of genius we mean as far as practicable, to supply its place with education," Stephen wrote Thompson. "I see no reason why our girls should receive a less thorough training than our boys."

Abby even overcame her usual stinginess with money. "Your father, as well as myself agree if you wish to take a four year course you can take it. The funds will be furnished. My own desire has always been that you should have as thorough an education as you can obtain," she wrote to Alla.

Alla, however, did not have a very high opinion of herself. "I am so proud of you and father, that you are both so devoted, according to your strength, to all reforms," she wrote Abby. "I am sure that I shall never do anything half so useful. But the children of good and great people are apt to be ugly and forceless, and I think you and I should be thankful that I am not any worse."

Her parents tried to inspire her with some of their enthusiasm for reform. When Alla wrote home complaining that students' rights were overlooked, Abby suggested that a small group leave the college as a protest. Alla answered that she didn't feel much would be accomplished by such an action.

"We think you entirely mistaken," Abby rejoined. "Should only one leave for good reason, and publish in a few respectable journals the reasons for so doing, it would effect ultimately, perhaps not immediately, a radical change."

Alla, however, had had enough of radical change in childhood. She took no stands, enlisted in no causes, but remained a good, though obscure, student throughout her Vassar years.

Abby's letters to Alla at college were warm, gossipy, and full of snippets about new clothes and Worcester news.

Various young girls were announcing their engagements, getting married, or having babies. Abby made it clear she thought Alla was well off to be out of the range of matrimony, at least for the time being.

Everyone was currently reading a book called *Little Women* published by Louisa May Alcott. "I saw Louisa Alcott when last in Boston and upbraided her for not allowing Jo to remain an old maid," Abby wrote in one of her letters to Vassar. "She replied that it was not her fault that she was married. She left her as should be in sublime maidenhood, blessing the whole world and being blessed in return—but her friends set up such a howl against it, and the publishers joining in the chorus, saying, it won't sell half as well, the change was inevitable. But by and by her old maid will come, she promises."

After graduating from Vassar in 1872, Alla became a teacher. She never married, and remained devoted to her parents, though the devotion may have been touched with a bit of resentment. Abby continued to worry about Alla's health, as she had when she was small, and to take great pleasure in her accomplishments. She was especially proud when Alla decided to go West to teach, as a protest against the unequal pay for men and women teachers prevailing in the East.

"Here even when men do no more and no better work than women and take no greater responsibility, they are sometimes paid three times as much," Abby wrote a friend.

All her life Abby had asserted her rights as a woman, rather than just talking about doing so. Going to women's rights meetings was all very well, but she continued to look for a way to make concrete her stand.

"Way opened," as Abby would say, in 1873, when she

heard about two Connecticut sisters, Abby and Julia Smith, of Glastonbury, who were refusing to pay taxes on their farm because they were not allowed to vote. This was taxation without representation, the sisters said.

Abby saw in a flash this was the right course for herself. It was in keeping with her Quaker ancestors, who had refused to pay war taxes, and with the nonresistance movement, of which she had so long been a part. She and Stephen had admired Henry Thoreau when he spent a night in jail rather than pay his poll tax to a government that was supporting the unpopular war in Mexico. Here was their chance to do likewise.

Stephen readily agreed, and they refused to pay their 1873 taxes. The city of Worcester waited a year, then seized the farm for unpaid taxes in 1874 and threatened to sell it over their heads to the highest bidder.

All the reform newspapers of the day carried the story, and Abby was once more in the full floodlight of notoriety. Old friends wrote from far and near to praise her action.

"Of course I need not tell either of you at this late day how much I appreciate this last chapter in lives full of heroic self sacrifice to conviction," Wendell Phillips commented.

"These sales of property are to the Woman's Suffrage movement what the fugitive slave cases were to the antislavery movement," Thomas Wentworth Higginson, a former neighbor, said. "Knowing as I do, the energy and patient industry by which you brought your farm into its present condition, 'putting,' as Mr. Garrison said, 'all your combativeness into the soil,' it seems to me a great sacrifice when you allow it to be sold."

Even Garrison broke fifteen years of silence to write Abby,

congratulating her on her courage. "Yours has been a life of self sacrifice in behalf of the downtrodden and oppressed. I offer you my heartfelt thanks and best wishes," he wrote.

With her old flair for getting as much mileage as possible out of an issue, Abby organized a "Convention on Taxation without Representation" to occur the day before the legal proceedings. Many of the old reformers came; others sent regards. Lucy Stone and her husband, Henry Blackwell, were there in spirit if not in body. Elizabeth Cady Stanton praised Abby's action. The old wounds of factionalism were healed.

"I hope there is not a man in your city or county, or elsewhere who will meanly seek to make that property available to his own selfish ends. Let there be no buyer at any price," Garrison had written.

Unfortunately, there was a buyer. On the morning of the sale, when the Fosters and their friends crowded into the tax office, a Tatnuck neighbor came forward and offered one hundred dollars for the farm. His name was Osgood Plummer, and he was evidently one of the bigots of whom Abby had complained when they first moved to Liberty Farm.

On the spot, Stephen gave him a tonguelashing. Plummer retreated, then wrote a letter to the Worcester *Spy* saying he had done it only to teach the Fosters a lesson in obeying the law.

The deed reverted to the city. The next year the Fosters were again delinquent in their taxes. The wrangle continued until 1880, with the Fosters paying several thousand not to lose their house, and Alla at times meeting the yearly tax bill. Finally Stephen, too ill to continue, settled up. By this time Abby's point had been made. By living with the anxiety and heartache of all but losing her beloved home, and watching their tiny life savings vanish, she had once more made smooth the path for others to follow.

Commenting on the case, Elizabeth Cady Stanton wrote that a proper adornment of the walls of the Woman's Pavilion at the 1876 Centennial would be "the papers issued by the city of Worcester for the forced sales of the house and lands of Abby Kelley Foster, the veteran abolitionist, because she refused to pay taxes, giving the same reason as our ancestors when they resisted taxation."

## XXII

# A Path Worn Smooth

In the 1870s most people still believed firmly in a life after death, as promised in the Bible. As they grew older, both Abby and Stephen began to think more about it.

Stephen for one was beginning to have his doubts. His religious faith itself began to crumble toward the end of his days. How could a just God put up with the presence of evil? It tortured his mind.

Abby, on the other hand, never lost her serene faith in the God within each person. It was an abstract principle—not a personal God, not the fatherly God in the attic—in which she now believed, but it gave her strength to face whatever trials came her way.

And yet of the two it was Stephen who acted more as though he believed that there was "that of God in everyone," Alla, their daughter, recalled. "My mother found it hard to like people with whom she differed, but my father loved everybody."

In 1876 Stephen had a stroke. After that he was never well.

Fearful that the Fosters might die without leaving a record of their exciting lives, William Henry Channing, an old friend and a journalist, wrote them a long letter begging them to dictate their memoirs to Alla, or to some other sympathetic friend.

"Among the many good, brave, true-hearted and clear sighted advocates of justice and mercy toward the enslaved, and of consistent loyalty to the Principles of our Republic few, if any, were prompted by a simpler and a keener, a purer and more persistent sense of duty than yourselves," he wrote. He intimated he regarded it as their duty now to preserve their experiences for posterity, and said he would leave it up to their Quaker and Puritan consciences respectively. If they would only let their memories bubble forth, he was sure that the resulting book would not only be of historic interest but would be inspiring, touching, and sometimes funny.

Abby had consistently refused, all her life, to write any autobiographical notes at all. In the 1850s a woman approached her with the request that she be allowed to write her biography, but Abby turned her down, indicating that she thought it would harm "the cause." Stephen had fewer inhibitions but found writing a chore. He evidently toyed with the idea of producing some memoirs, for he wrote to several old friends asking for documents. Nevertheless, the book which Channing proposed was never written. For many years, Abby and Stephen were lost to history.

The old guard was thinning, the old days slipping away into the mists. Parker Pillsbury wrote from his travels in the West that he was amazed to find people who had scarcely heard about "the thirty years war," even a few who didn't recognize the name of Abby Kelley Foster!

There was need of a new generation of reformers, for Reconstruction in the South was as dismal a failure as Abby had predicted. The Ku Klux Klan arose to deprive the blacks of that right to vote for which she had fought so passionately. The spirit of reform seemed dead. No one cared.

"Since the government does not subscribe to peace principles it ought to send troops into the South to protect the helpless blacks," Abby wrote in a passionate letter in the *Standard*. When William Lloyd Garrison protested Rutherford B. Hayes's "conciliatory policy" toward the Southern states in the New York *Times*, she supported him warmly.

"We are now seeing the slave oligarchy in the Republican party," she pointed out, doubtless thinking of Garrison's enthusiastic support of that party during the Civil War. "My husband wishes me to add that the deepest regret he has in losing his health is that he cannot join in the work of turning the tide, now setting against the freedmen."

The letter broke what ice remained between Garrison and Abby. He asked her to furnish some material in a quarrel he was having with Parker Pillsbury. In return, he wrote at her request to the *Woman's Journal* to correct the statement that the American Anti-Slavery Society had split over a "side issue" when Abby's election to a committee caused the New Organization to withdraw. The defense of their common cause in the distant past was still passionately important to them both.

In May 1879, Garrison died. His death was a major shock to Abby. Friend or foe, he had been one of the most important influences on her life ever since she was twenty-five. It seemed impossible that such a giant could pass from the scene.

The early reformers had not spared themselves, and they

died early. In 1880, when the thirtieth anniversary of the first women's rights convention was held, only Abby Kelley Foster and Lucy Stone were left from the original group that had met in Worcester in 1850. When Abby and Lucy stepped on the platform together, their appearance was met with thunderous applause. Reference was made to Abby's famous "bloody feet" speech. Samuel May, Thomas Wentworth Higginson, and other old friends offered congratulations. The news of the death of Lydia Maria Child added a note of sadness to a joyous occasion.

Abby herself was not strong and suffered from nose and throat ailments. Her problems were mild, however, compared to Stephen's. By 1878 he had become an invalid. Thereafter he longed for the release of death. His old friends Parker Pillsbury and Wendell Phillips wrote him cheering letters, but the only thing that would really have cheered him would be to be up and about, crusading again. Knowing how he felt, Abby must have felt some consolation at his release when, on September 8, 1881, he died.

Letters of sympathy to Abby and tribute to Stephen poured in from everywhere. The Garrison children wrote lovingly on their memories of the farm. Frederick Douglass talked about Stephen's contribution to the end of slavery. Old friends from the Ohio and Pennsylvania campaigns spoke of his influence on their lives.

At the memorial service held in his honor in Worcester, Lucy Stone, Parker Pillsbury, and Wendell Phillips all spoke. The old, frail Stephen was forgotten; his youthful, thundering self alone remembered. "It needed something to shake New England and stun it into listening," Wendell Phillips said. "He was the man, and offered himself for the martyrdom."

Still vigorous, Parker Pillsbury went home with his head full of memories of his old comrade. The result was the publication, several years later, of a book, *The Acts of the Anti-Slavery Apostles,* telling the story of Stephen's early experiences in interrupting church services.

Abby was a philosopher, skilled at facing and accepting the inevitable. Forty years ago she had met Stephen. From that day to this her life had been bound up with his. But now Stephen was gone, and life must somehow continue. Shortly thereafter she sold her farm and moved in to Worcester to live with her younger sister, Lucy Barton.

After all her years of hard work, Abby now at last had leisure. There was time to read, to write letters, to visit old friends. Alla, back East now in nearby Boston, came for weekends and took her mother for vacations to the mountains and the sea. It should have been a time of peacefulness.

Unfortunately, there were minor irritations. Abby's eyes began to bother her. Alla suggested knitting as a way to keep busy without eyestrain. Abby's nose and throat problems grew worse, and she kept a spitbox at her side at all times. Lucy's other boarders complained about the spitbox, and about Abby's habit of washing her teeth in public. Lucy spoke to Alla, and Alla gave her mother a gentle, condescending lecture about her personal habits.

Abby bore these indignities of old age stoically. The only thing she worried about was losing the use of her mind. She felt that she was growing forgetful, and complained about the behavior of her poor flickering brain.

In fact, however, she remained keen and alert. She kept up a lively interest in current events. At the time of the election of 1884 she decided she was willing to have the Democrats replace the Republicans and thus give the party long in power a chance for a housecleaning. Though she preferred the Republicans, recent scandals had dismayed her.

She was also interested in Gladstone, the prime minister of England, and followed his doings in the paper.

> I consider Gladstone a remarkable statesman if statesmanship consists in carrying a government forward, with gradual improvement, and with as little friction as great qualities of foresight, wisdom, and prudence will allow. He is evidently satisfied with the correctness of democratic principles, and will do all in his power to introduce them as fast as it can be done without revolution. But he must vote . . . for consistency's sake and to keep Victoria and her class quiet. And a great many other things too, which he can but condemn in his own soul as great wrongs. No person can be a real follower of Christ and be a statesman. The real Christian will be crusified [sic] all the day long, and life long, if life is spared.

In the early summer of 1886 Lucy Stone decided to arrange a reunion of oldtimers. Abby's oldest friend, Elizabeth Buffum Chace, was there, as well as Samuel May, the four sons of William Lloyd Garrison, Theodore Weld, and many others. Abby was well enough to enjoy the occasion thoroughly, and her friends thought she looked better than she had for years.

The year before she had finally given in to constant requests and written a small portion of her memoirs. She worked without notes, and when her stories are checked against earlier newspaper accounts, they are often inaccurate. Nevertheless, she worked hard to bring lost memories to the surface and felt pleased with the results.

Perhaps on the strength of this experience she decided in the late fall to attempt a short sketch of Stephen for the *Cyclopedia of Biography*. Though the entry was to be brief she went to enormous pains to make it absolutely accurate. She asked Parker Pillsbury to help, and she consulted old records. Her sister and her friends began to notice that she went at the work with an odd intensity. It was her last chance to vindicate Stephen and those ideas for which the two of them had fought for so long. In the process of remembering, she relived the many battles they had been through together.

"Her sister, Mrs. Barton, saw the effect on her—begged her to go more slowly—to spare herself; again and again tried to have her take her rest," Samuel May wrote to a friend. "I suppose she could not; the duty, once undertaken . . . would impel her to go on, without stopping, to completion. It even seems strange to me that she lived to complete it."

But complete it she did. Only after the copy had gone to the printers did she allow herself to relax. She went to her bed that night in a state of exhaustion from which she never recovered. Two days later, on January 14, 1887, she died.

The funeral was small, and private, but Lucy Stone, William Lloyd Garrison, Jr., and Samuel May all spoke. Obituaries appeared in the *Nation* and the Boston *Daily Advertiser*, as well as the local paper. Her friend Elizabeth Buffum Chace prepared a tribute which was published in the *Woman's Journal* in March: "The women of this land owe to this woman, more than to any other human being, a debt of gratitude for the doors she opened for them to enter, for the paths she made smooth for them with her own bleeding feet, for the courage and the conscientiousness and the faithfulness with which, amid persecution and reviling, she made the way clear for them to walk safely," she wrote.

Several years later Alla was asked to read some reminiscences of her mother at the fortieth anniversary of the first national woman's rights convention. She spoke of Abby's simplicity, determination, cheerfulness, and unselfconsciousness; her lack of humor; her inability to keep a secret; her faith.

> Those who listened to Abby Kelley in the days of her young womanhood have told me of her wonderful power. This consisted, I imagine, chiefly in her intense earnestness, in her utter self forgetfulness and consecration. Her language was of Quaker simplicity, unadorned with figures of imagery; she never wrote her speeches, and rarely spent any time in their preparation; but the eloquence of a heart on fire, words lighted at the altar of God's truth, were hers. Her audience felt that she "remembered those in bonds as bound with them." Such a passion for freedom, such unselfish devotion, could not fail to inspire admiration and to win converts.

If Abby had been there, she might have reminded Alla wryly that her passion for freedom had also inspired anger and won her enemies. But times had changed, and the old taunt of *Jezebel* was forgotten. Women could speak in public now, and no one challenged them. For generations to come, Abby had made smooth the path.

# Suggested Further Reading

Cromwell, Otelia. *Lucretia Mott*. Cambridge, Harvard University Press, 1958.

Flexner, Eleanor. *Century of Struggle: The Woman's Rights Movement in the United States*. Cambridge, Belknap Press, 1959.

Hayes, Eleanor. *Morning Star: A Biography of Lucy Stone*. New York, Harcourt, Brace & World, 1961.

Lader, Lawrence. *The Bold Brahmins: New England's War Against Slavery 1831–1863*. New York, E. P. Dutton & Company, 1961.

Lerner, Gerda. *The Grimké Sisters from South Carolina: Rebels Against Slavery*. Boston, Houghton Mifflin, 1967.

Lutz, Alma. *Susan B. Anthony, Rebel, Crusader, Humanitarian*. Boston, Beacon Press, 1959.

McConnell, Jane T. *Cornelia: The Story of a Civil War Nurse*. New York, Thomas Y. Crowell, 1959.

Meltzer, Milton. *Tongue of Flame: The Life of Lydia Maria Child*. New York, Thomas Y. Crowell, 1965.

Merrill, Walter M. *Against Wind & Tide: A Biography of William Lloyd Garrison*. Cambridge, Harvard University Press, 1963.

Riegel, Robert E. *American Feminists.* Lawrence, University of Kansas Press, 1963.

Sterling, Dorothy. *Lucretia Mott: Gentle Warrior.* Garden City, N.Y., Doubleday & Co., 1965.

Yates, Elizabeth. *Prudence Crandall: Woman of Courage.* New York, E. P. Dutton, 1955.

# Bibliography

## MANUSCRIPT COLLECTIONS CONSULTED

Blackwell Family Papers. Library of Congress
Foster Papers. American Antiquarian Society. Worcester, Mass.
Foster Papers. Worcester Historical Society. Worcester, Mass.
Garrison Papers. Boston Public Library
Sydney Howard Gay Papers. Columbia University
Samuel May Papers. Boston Public Library
Lucretia Mott Papers. Swarthmore College
Elizabeth Cady Stanton Papers. Library of Congress
Records, Friends School in Providence. New England Yearly
    Meeting Archives
Records, Friends School in Lynn. New England Yearly Meeting
    Archives
Records, Uxbridge Monthly Meeting. New England Yearly Meet-
    ing Archives

## PERIODICALS

*Liberator*, 1831–1865
*National Anti-Slavery Standard*, 1840–1870

*New England Magazine*, January 1903, "Reminiscences of Two Abolitionists." Lillian Buffum Chace Wyman

*Woman's Journal*, February 7, 1871, "Reminiscences of Abby Kelley Foster." Alla Foster

*Quakeriana Notes*, November 6, 1936

*Journal of American History*, March 1972, "Confrontation and Abolition in 1850's." Jane and William Pease

*Germantown Crier*, Winter 1971, "The Night They Burned Pennsylvania Hall." Margaret H. Bacon


## BOOKS

Baer, Helene G. *The Heart Is Like Heaven: The Life of Lydia Maria Child.* Philadelphia, University of Pennsylvania Press, 1964.

Chace, Elizabeth Buffum. *Anti-Slavery Reminiscences.* Central Falls, R.I., Fremont & Sons, 1891.

Coolidge, Louise. *An Old Fashioned Senator: Orville Platt of Connecticut.* New York, Putnam and Sons, 1910.

Drake, Thomas. *Quakers and Slavery in America.* New Haven, Yale University Press, 1950.

Emerson, Sarah Hopper. *The Life of Abby Hopper Gibbons, as told in her letters.* 2 volumes. New York, G. P. Putnam, 1897.

Garrison. *William Lloyd Garrison. His Life as told by his children.* 4 volumes. New York, The Century Company, 1885–1889.

Kraditor, Aileen S. *Means and Ends in American Abolitionism.* New York, Random House, 1969.

Lynd, Staughton. *Nonviolence in America.* Indianapolis, Bobbs-Merrill Co., 1966.

McPherson, James. *The Struggle for Equality.* Princeton, Princeton University Press, 1964.

Pease, Jane. *The Freshness of Fanaticism, Abby Kelley Foster, An Essay in Reform.* The University of Rochester, 1969, unprinted Ph.D. thesis.

Pease, Jane and William. *Bound with Them in Chains.* Westport, Conn., Greenwood Press, 1972.

Pillsbury, Parker. *The Acts of the Anti-Slavery Apostles.* New Hampshire, Clague Wegman Schlict & Co. 1883.

Powell, Aaron. *Personal Reminiscences of the Anti-Slavery and Other Reforms and Reformers.* New York, Cavlon Press, 1899.

O'Connor, Lillian. *Pioneer Women Orators.* New York, Columbia University Press, 1954.

Robinson, Harriet. *Massachusetts in the Woman Suffrage Movement.* Boston, Roberts Brothers, 1883.

Stanton, Elizabeth Cady, et al. *History of Woman Suffrage.* 3 volumes. New York, Fowler and Wells, 1881.

Stanton. *Eighty Years or More: Reminiscences of Elizabeth Cady Stanton.* New York, European Publishing Company, 1898.

Wyman, Lillian Buffum Chace. *Elizabeth Buffum Chace and Her Environment.* 2 volumes. Boston, W. B. Clarke Co., 1914.


PAMPHLETS

*The Brotherhood of Thieves, or a True Picture of the American Church and Clergy.* New London, Wm. Bolles, 1843.

*The History of Pennsylvania Hall, which was burned by a mob on the 17th of May, 1838.* Philadelphia, Merrihew and Gunn, 1838.

*The Underground Railroad in Massachusetts.* Wilbur H. Siebert, Reprinted from the Proceedings of the American Antiquarian Society, April 1935, Worcester, 1936.

# *Index*

Foster, Stephen S. (*cont.*):
  and Abby Kelley, 73, 95–103,
    105–106, 107, 110–111,
    113–114, 118
  and abolition movement, 70–
    74, 95–96, 121–122, 126–
    130, 148–150, 152, 162–
    163, 173–174, 175, 179–
    180, 187–197, 206
  attacks on clergy, 70–74, 101,
    113–114, 127, 208
  death, 217–218
  marriage, 122–125, 135–139,
    151, 152, 153, 175–176
  and nonresistance, 130–132,
    163, 165, 167–170, 177,
    187, 206
  and other reform movements,
    207–208, 211–212
  and political action, 101–
    102, 127, 130, 148–149,
    177–178, 182, 184, 188–
    189
  and suffrage, 198–205, 211–
    212
  and women's rights move-
    ment, 157, 198–204, 208,
    211
Fourteenth Amendment, 198
Free Produce Movement, 31
Free Soil Party, 148, 176, 178,
  188
Free Will Baptists, 75
Frémont, John, 181, 196
Friends, *see* Quakers

Friends School, The (Providence, Rhode Island), 11,
  13
Fugitive Slave Law, 159, 163,
  166, 189

Garrett, Thomas, 110
Garrison, James, 171
Garrison, William Lloyd, 23,
  31, 32, 47, 48, 49, 54, 69,
  73, 78, 85, 88, 96, 139, 166–
  167, 172, 173, 178, 181,
  182, 184–186, 195, 196,
  211–212, 216
  attacks on clergy, 27, 36, 68
  and colonization scheme, 17–
    19
  and nonresistance, 40–43, 188
  and political action, 42, 181,
    191–192, 193
  and women's rights, 26–27,
    36, 55–58
Garrisonians, 38, 40, 41, 48, 49,
  50, 55–58, 61, 68, 69, 78,
  82, 86, 100, 101–102, 108,
  140, 177–179, 189, 190,
  192, 193, 196–197
Gay, Sydney Howard, 112, 120,
  124, 140, 194
*Genius of Universal Emancipa-
  tion, The*, 17
Gibbons, James, 84
Giddings, Joshua, 91, 116, 117,
  119
Gladstone, William Ewart, 219
Graham, Sylvester, 21

## ABOUT THE AUTHOR

When Margaret Hope Bacon was growing up, her father, an artist, illustrated many children's books. Mrs. Bacon says that she cannot remember a time when she did not intend to write such books herself someday.

Her research for this biography of Abby Kelley Foster led her to Abby's various homes in Worcester and Mendon, Massachusetts; to the little meeting in Uxbridge, from which she was disowned; and to the American Antiquarian Society and the Worcester Historical Society, which hold some five hundred of her letters.

Mrs. Bacon grew up in New York City, went to high school in Florida, and was graduated from Antioch College in Ohio. She and her husband now live in Philadelphia, where she is a writer for the American Friends Service Committee. In addition to I SPEAK FOR MY SLAVE SISTER, she is the author of *Lamb's Warrior: The Life of Isaac T. Hopper;* a history of American Quakers, *The Quiet Rebels;* and a book about black resistance to slavery, *Rebellion at Christiana.*